they call me
DOC

they call me DOC

THE STORY BEHIND
THE LEGEND OF
JOHN HENRY HOLLIDAY

D. J. HERDA

LYONS PRESS
Guilford, Connecticut

Lyons Press is an imprint of Globe Pequot Press.

Project editor: David Legere
Text design: Maggie Peterson
Layout: Sue Murray

Library of Congress Cataloging-in-Publication Data is available on file.

ISBN 978-0-7627-6046-6

Printed in the United States of America

Distributed by NATIONAL BOOK NETWORK

To Big Nose Kate, who led me to Doc,
and to Mimi, who led me to
everything else.

CONTENTS

Preface   ix

Introduction: A Moment in Time   xi

1   Speaking Out   1

2   A Man Called Doc   9

3   War!   16

4   The End of Innocence   29

5   Love, Death, Betrayal, Etc.   38

6   The Doctor Is In   44

7   Affirmations   55

8   The Deadliest Dentist   59

9   Westward Bound   64

10   My Darling Whore   80

11   Vendetta's Edge   93

12   A Town Called Tombstone   108

13   Thief in the Night   117

14   Shootout at the O.K. Corral   128

15   A Shot in the Dark   143

16   Rough Riders   150

17   One Last Goodbye   165

Epilogue   177

Index   180

About the Author   189

PREFACE

When I sat down to begin researching my biography on one of the least known and least written about figures of the Old West, Doc Holliday was far from my mind. I was searching for material that would lead me to a book about a woman named Kate Harony, otherwise known as "Big Nose" Kate. As I struggled to find what bits and pieces I could about Doc's lifelong paramour, I began to despair. Precious little had been recorded about the woman over the passage of time.

And then I felt a light tap on my shoulder, followed by a simple thought entering my mind: *I'll tell you everything you want to know about Kate if you'll write my story first. The* real *story. The story of Doctor John H. Holliday.*

It was not the first time I had been contacted by a historical figure from the grave. It also happened to me while researching former Supreme Court Justice Earl Warren. After I had completed the book, my publisher sent it to Earl Warren Jr., Warren's son and a sitting judge in California. Junior politely declined to endorse it, saying that he had made it a lifelong policy never to comment upon anything written about his deceased father.

Several days later, Junior wrote my publisher and said that he'd changed his mind, calling the book the best biography he'd ever read about his dad. "The author knew things he couldn't possibly have known. He would have had to have been seated around the dinner table with the rest of the family to know some of those things. I don't know how he did it, but I will wholeheartedly endorse this book."

I didn't realize it at the time, but Warren had been feeding me the truth, the real story of oft-maligned Earl Warren Senior, directing my writing as he did.

A similar thing happened to me in researching other biographies— one of Ernest Hemingway and another of Dorothy Parker. When it happened yet again, this time with Doc calling the shots, it suddenly dawned on me . . . this really was his tale.

And so my biography of Doc Holliday was born, and I bring it to the world as a personal tribute and a singular testimony to the morals, the scruples, and the impeccable manners of a true southern gentleman.

I am pleased to present my biography of Doctor John H. Holliday to the world in order to set the record straight.

In his very own words.

Introduction
A Moment in Time

YESTERDAY'S TRAGEDY

Tombstone Daily Epitaph, *October 27, 1881*

THREE MEN HURLED INTO ETERNITY IN THE DURATION
OF A MOMENT

S tormy as were the early days of Tombstone nothing
ever occurred equal to the event of yesterday. Since the
retirement of Ben Sippy as marshal and the appointment
of V. W. Earp to fill the vacancy the town has been noted for
its quietness and good order. The fractious and much dreaded
Cowboys when they came to town were upon their good
behaviour and no unseemly brawls were indulged in, and it was
hoped by our citizens that no more such deeds would occur as
led to the killing of Marshal White one year ago. It seems that
this quiet state of affairs was but the calm that precedes the
storm that burst in all its fury yesterday, with this difference
in results, that the lightning bolt struck in a different quarter
from the one that fell a year ago. This time it struck with its
full and awful force upon those who, heretofore, have made the
good name of this county a byword and a reproach, instead of
upon some officer in discharge of his duty or a peaceable and
unoffending citizen.

Since the arrest of Stilwell and Spencer for the robbery of
the Bisbee stage, there have been oft repeated threats conveyed

to the Earp brothers—Virgil, Morgan and Wyatt—that the friends of the accused, or in other words the Cowboys, would get even with them for the part they had taken in the pursuit and arrest of Stilwell and Spence. The active part of the Earps in going after stage robbers, beginning with the one last spring where Budd Philpot lost his life, and the more recent one near Contention, has made them exceedingly obnoxious to the bad element of this county and put their lives in jeopardy every month.

Sometime Tuesday Ike Clanton came into town and during the evening had some little talk with Doc Holliday and Marshal Earp but nothing to cause either to suspect, further than their general knowledge of the man and the threats that had previously been conveyed to the Marshal, that the gang intended to clean out the Earps, that he was thirsting for blood at this time with one exception and that was that Clanton told the Marshal, in answer to a question, that the McLowrys [*sic*] were in Sonora. Shortly after this occurrence someone came to the Marshal and told him that the McLowrys [*sic*] had been seen a short time before just below town. Marshal Earp, now knowing what might happen and feeling his responsibility for the peace and order of the city, stayed on duty all night and added to the police force his brother Morgan and Holliday. The night passed without any disturbance whatever and at sunrise he went home to rest and sleep. A short time afterwards one of his brothers came to his house and told him that Clanton was hunting him with threats of shooting him on sight. He discredited the report and did not get out of bed. It was not long before another of his brothers came down, and told him the same thing, whereupon he got up, dressed and went with his brother Morgan uptown. They walked up Allen Street to Fifth, crossed over to Fremont and down to Fourth, where, upon turning up Fourth toward Allen, they came upon Clanton with a Winchester rifle in his hand and a revolver on his hip.

The Marshal walked up to him, grabbed the rifle and hit him a blow on the head at the same time, stunning him so that he was able to disarm him without further trouble. He marched Clanton off to the police court where he entered a complaint against him for carrying deadly weapons, and the court fined Clanton $25 and costs, making $27.50 altogether. This occurrence must have been about 1 o'clock in the afternoon.

THE AFTER-OCCURRENCE

Close upon the heels of this came the finale, which is best told in the words of R. F. Coleman, who was an eyewitness from the beginning to the end. Mr. Coleman says:

"I was in the O.K. Corral at 2:30 p.m., when I saw the two Clantons and the two McLowrys [sic] in an earnest conversation across the street in Dunbar's corral. I went up the street and notified Sheriff Behan and told him it was my opinion they meant trouble, and it was his duty, as sheriff, to go and disarm them. I told him they had gone to the West End Corral. I then went and saw Marshal Virgil Earp and notified him to the same effect. I then met Billy Allen and we walked through the O.K. Corral, about fifty yards behind the sheriff. On reaching Fremont Street I saw Virgil Earp, Wyatt Earp, Morgan Earp and Doc Holliday, in the center of the street, all armed. I had reached Bauer's meat market. Johnny Behan had just left the Cowboys, after having a conversation with them. I went along to Fly's photograph gallery, when I heard Virg Earp say, 'Give up your arms or throw up your arms.' There was some reply made by Frank McLowry [sic], when firing became general, over thirty shots being fired. Tom McLowry [sic] fell first, but raised and fired again before he died. Bill Clanton fell next, and raised to fire again when Mr. Fly took his revolver from him. Frank McLowry [sic] ran a few rods and fell. Morgan Earp was shot through and fell. Doc Holliday was hit in the left hip but kept on firing.

Virgil Earp was hit in the third or fourth fire, in the leg which staggered him but he kept up his effective work. Wyatt Earp stood up and fired in rapid succession, as cool as a cucumber, and was not hit. Doc Holliday was as calm as though at target practice and fired rapidly. After the firing was over, Sheriff Behan went up to Wyatt Earp and said, 'I'll have to arrest you.' Wyatt replied: 'I won't be arrested today. I am right here and am not going away. You have deceived me. You told me these men were disarmed; I went to disarm them.'"

This ends Mr. Coleman's story which in the most essential particulars has been confirmed by others. Marshal Earp says that he and his party met the Clantons and the McLowrys [sic] in the alleyway by the McDonald place; he called to them to throw up their hands, that he had come to disarm them. Instantaneously Bill Clanton and one of the McLowrys [sic] fired, and then it became general. Mr. Earp says it was the first shot from Frank McLowry [sic] that hit him. In other particulars his statement does not materially differ from the statement above given. Ike Clanton was not armed and ran across to Allen Street and took refuge in the dance hall there. The two McLowrys [sic] and Bill Clanton all died within a few minutes after being shot. The Marshal was shot through the calf of the right leg, the ball going clear through. His brother, Morgan, was shot through the shoulders, the ball entering the point of the right shoulder blade, following across the back, shattering off a piece of one vertebrae and passing out the left shoulder in about the same position that it entered the right. The wound is dangerous but not necessarily fatal, and Virgil's is far more painful than dangerous. Doc Holliday was hit upon the scabbard of his pistol, the leather breaking the force of the ball so that no material damage was done other than to make him limp a little in his walk.

Dr. Matthews impaneled a coroner's jury, who went and viewed the bodies as they lay in the cabin in the rear of Dunbar's stables on Fifth Street, and then adjourned until 10 o'clock this morning.

THE ALARM GIVEN

The moment the word of the shooting reached the Vizina and Tough Nut mines the whistles blew a shrill signal, and the miners came to the surface, armed themselves, and poured into the town like an invading army. A few moments served to bring out all the better portions of the citizens, thoroughly armed and ready for any emergency. Precautions were immediately taken to preserve law and order, even if they had to fight for it. A guard of ten men were stationed around the county jail, and extra policemen put on for the night.

EARP BROTHERS JUSTIFIED

The feeling among the best class of our citizens is that the Marshal was entirely justified in his efforts to disarm these men, and that being fired upon they had to defend themselves, which they did most bravely. So long as our peace officers make an effort to preserve the peace and put down highway robbery—which the Earp brothers have done, having engaged in the pursuit and capture, where captures have been made of every gang of stage robbers in the county—they will have the support of all good citizens. If the present lesson is not sufficient to teach the Cowboy element that they can not come into the streets of Tombstone, in broad daylight, armed with six shooters and Henry rifles to hunt down their victims, then the citizens will most assuredly take such steps to preserve the peace as will be forever a bar to such raids.

Speaking Out

A lot of people have written about me these past five score years and more since my untimely demise. A lot of people have said things, and a lot of people have been wrong.

Not that I blame them.

When you have lived as colorful and, as some might say, sordid a life as I, and when you have been gone from center stage for so long a period as I, things are bound to go a bit bug-eyed from time to time.

Still, I have seen people refer to me as though they knew me. As such, they have portrayed me as a cold-blooded killer and a heartless, homeless wretch, as a whoring whirl-a-way and a confidence man and even—if you can believe it—a drunk.

Me. Can you imagine?

And of course there is all this talk about me being a lunger. *Sick* and emaciated, a walking wheezing wobbling wretch of a human being. A man of gray hair and gaunt complexion though barely in his thirties.

That last part, of course, is undeniably true. And probably the part about the drunk. At least so far as I can recall. And maybe a little about the whoring whirl-a-way. But a confidence man? A heartless wretch? A cold-blooded killer? *Me?* Are they kidding me?

I have spent my life looking for good and eschewing evil. I have searched the world over for the best in humanity and stood up to the worst. I have looked down the gullet of perdition and reached out to embrace salvation.

Call me the way, the light, and the truth. I am the reincarnation of the Son of our God, Lord Jesus Christ.

Oh, don't take that as blasphemy. I am not Jesus, nor do I pretend to be him. There is one blessed Lord and one son, the Lord our God, and, unfortunately for me, I am *not* him.

No, what I mean when I say that I am the soul, the very reincarnation, of the Lord is that I would have liked him, had I lived in a much earlier period of time. And I am convinced, not too contrarily, that he would have liked me as well. Liked me so much, perhaps, that he would have imbued within me those very honorable and lofty traits upon which he was bestowed by his father.

I say this not so much out of fanciful conjecture as out of the study of mankind and humanity, in all its frailty and weakness, versus the glorious revelations of the supreme being: He would have found in me a soul so eager to please, so destined to emulate, so desirous of satisfying those demands he placed upon us humans that I would literally have carried the cross in place of him up from the town of Judea to the barren fields known as Golgotha and when it came time to strip him of his robes and boost him into his place of everlasting life, would gladly have exchanged positions with him.

And with that lofty feeling firmly entrenched within my own pasty white, frail, all-too-human entity, I went forth into life, set upon doing his work in his name for his glory and without but a glance back at what was in it for me. For the way, the truth, and the Kingdom are one in the name of the Lord within me. Or at least they were in the latter part of my miserable and wretched little life.

True, I may have overreacted upon rare occasion and lost sight of my goals, particularly when having been exposed to the languid effects of too much fine Tennessee sipping whiskey and the stupidity and cowardliness of some of the bullies I have come up against during my lifetime of precocious morbidity, but that is little reason to fault my motives. They have always been pure, I can assure you, oftentimes in direct contradiction to the popular word wending its way along the walk.

And for those times when I did manage to stray from my greater purpose in life, well, I have paid the price, let me assure you. And I apologize. That is another thing I have never been remembered for—my boundless capacity for contrition. And that is another thing I intend to right.

I have wanted to set the record straight for some time, of course. And I have attempted to do just that from as long ago as I can recall. First with Kate, thinking that she would be the ideal bearer of my sword; but Kate was in a world all her own, bless the darling loving, scheming, conniving little whore. She was far too busy looking after her own selfish interests to pay much attention to voices from the grave. Kate actually sought to cash in on me as her intimate and, some might say, upon her inspirational relationship with yours truly in exchange for cold, hard cash. Her eight pieces of silver? She would have succeeded, too, had she not been so damned blessed greedy about the whole stinking affair or had she not overestimated other peoples' desires to pay for the privilege of learning about me from the woman who had stood by me, by most accounts, for lo those many years. Had I known then what I know now, I would have gladly kicked the slut out of my life after that first soulless night, the moment her knickers fell to the floor and she dampened the light for her most dastardly and lascivious of purposes, if truth be known.

But I didn't, believing in the very bottom of my heart that she could be rehabilitated by the love of a good man.

Unfortunately, I was wrong.

Had she not turned out to be so insatiably greedy and not sought out the most exorbitant price she thought she could possibly wrangle for her own intimate tell-all tales of her life and times with the legendary gunfighter who went by the name of Doc Holliday, I might have found her receptive to my cries in time of need. I might have been able to reach out and touch her, move her, and in turn be able to rely upon her, even from the hereafter. I might have been able to approach her, awaken in her the spirit that I tried to instill in her while I was still alive. But then she would simply not have been Kate. I realized that when I met her. And I realize it still to this day.

Alas, Kate is no good to me now. She cannot help me right the record now. It is too late for that now.

My good friend Wyatt—to whom I shall always be grateful for the kind words he uttered upon my demise and for the stories he wrote and distributed by virtue of those most fine and honorable gentlemen of the press and for his undeviating devotion as a good friend and confidant throughout the latter years of my life—did what he could to set the record straight. He wrote and traveled and talked and answered those few kindhearted souls who remembered to ask him about not only the Clantons and the McLowrys [sic] and Johnny Ringo and Johnny Behan but also about his good and faithful and devoted friend, Doc. Old Doc. Old belligerent, caustic, itching-for-a-fight Doc.

But even the Earps had little actual knowledge of who I really was and what my life was really like and what happened inside of me when they were not around to act as witness and what I did when in the darkened twilight of my final days I found myself alone . . . and unprepared.

Besides, Wyatt had his own problems. Split between his genuine love for Mattie and the smoldering fire he felt within his soul (not to mention his loins) for Josie—and an even stronger bond I can personally assure you for each of the brothers that remained after the fight—I am continually amazed that he lived another score beyond me, and then some. By all that is holy and by all that is right, he should have died a dozen times before me. But by the grace of Almighty God he did not, and he lived on. But Wyatt, poor torn soul that he was from the very first day I laid eyes upon him, had other problems. Wyatt had the problems of the universe laid upon him. I am not sure to this day why that was. But I do know that he was the single most personally preoccupied soul I have ever known in my life. And perhaps that is one of the reasons for our bond. I am probably the second. You can play with the numbers and do the mathematics, but it all comes out the same: Wyatt did all that he could while he could, and that was not enough to stem the flow.

If I digress, forgive me. I am like the proverbial child at the candy counter. I can hardly believe my good fortune. At last, I must impress upon you, I have found my outlet. And the foul words attributed to my life and death shall no longer go unabated.

Not that everything has been a dastardly blur. Not on your life. I believe with every breath within me that I did actually come out of a coma, as some have reported, right there in that bed in Glenwood Springs, Colorado, and I believe I remember saying something to the effect of "This is funny," which people took to mean that I had never intended to die with my boots off. That I had looked down at my feet and saw my toes and that I said those by-now immortal words. That was the shootist's credo during my day, you understand.

You die with your boots on, and you die ready for action, ready for a fight, ready to right those wrongs against you, ready for anything. You die with your boots on, and you die with honor, standing up for what you believe in to the very end. You die with your boots on, and you die true to your own moral code.

You get caught with your boots off, on the other hand, and you have retired for the rest of the day or the week or your life or whatever it is and are no longer as well prepared as you might have been, or perhaps even *should* have been, to handle life as it comes at you, both barrels blazing. And that is precisely what happens when things are most likely to go all haywire.

I might have said those words when I awoke in the hotel room that day, and they might have ushered forth from these two trembling lips upon my realizing that my death was imminent and that I was ill-prepared for it and that I never should have allowed things to regress so far.

But just think about *that* for a moment.

Think about a man who has suffered from consumption all his life, from the time he had barely become an adult until his final breath on earth, and tell me how likely it would be that such a man would look down at his feet and think anything he might find there funny, as if surprised that he should have come to this junction in life.

Tell me that he would anticipate the arrival of death, perhaps within seconds, with surprise and resigned amusement, in precisely the same way that a farmer would anticipate the coming of a big storm—matter-of-factly, inevitably—and I will tell you that you do not understand the nature of the human soul very well.

No, like the farmer who fights the onset of the blow with every breath he can muster, when you live with death hovering over you for all of your adult life, you do not anticipate its inevitable arrival, find that arrival amusing, and then succumb to its allure. You fight it. You fight it with all your might. You fight it with everything you have at your disposal, because you have faced it down before, fought it before, Demon Death, and won. A dozen times. A hundred. Perhaps a thousand. You lose count along the way, you have fought it so often. You lose count, but you never lose hope, and you never stop fighting, and certainly not long enough to look down at your toes and utter, "This is funny," because you expected to die with your boots on.

The truth is you never expected to die at all. You never lose your determination to join the battle yet one more time and, yet one more time, emerge victorious. *Ingredior non in vereor:* Walk not in fear.

No, when those words or something very similar to them fell from my lips only moments before I passed out of one world and into the alluring boundaries of another, I meant nothing so flippant or so conceitedly cavalier as to what others have ascribed my intent. I have never been so glib.

What I would have meant had I uttered those immortal words was that, after all those years of battling death for the right to take yet one more breath deep into this trembling soul, I should awaken at death's door to find my only companion to be my two stockinged feet. Me, Doc Holliday, with friends and relatives spread across the entire length and breath of this great land of ours, with enemies even more in abundance and more widely strewn, that I should spend my final moments on earth in the company not of my good friend Wyatt or the woman with whom I had shared so much and fought so vehemently, Kate, but with instead these ten toes that were with me from the start. These ten toes that first must have been no larger around than a snap bean. These toes that have accompanied me through life and now helped me to usher that life out.

Tell me *that* is not funny.

Of course, other stories have been written about me as well—flattering, jack-asinine, self-serving, rarely accurate stories—in one book, in one newspaper report, in one magazine article after another. My own kin several generations removed have struggled to write about the real Doc Holliday and what *really* motivated me.

Why, that is purely preposterous.

I also read the other day about a relative of Ike Clanton—yes, we have information available to us here, all of us, in a sort—who was castigating me and my friend Wyatt Earp and Wyatt's brothers for our onerous and unwarranted actions at the gunfight at the corral that day and absolving that vexatious scoundrel from any wrongdoing in the matter. I do not know, I tell you, which is to be more pitied, more feared, or more reviled—the relative who writes falsehoods in your defense or the enemy who writes them in your demise. Both are scurrilous curs deserving of no kudos. On that you have my word.

So it is for precisely such reasons as the meaning behind those dying words uttered upon my brief hospital quarantine and for the malignant fallacies of well-meaning apologists and ill-meaning scoundrels and a thousand rumors circulated about me and my friends and consorts that I have been searching for a loquacious manner by which to right the wrongs, to tell the true story, to offer for examination all of the rebuttals to all of the libelous and scandalous tall tales ever written about me, told by so many people in so many corners of the world over so very many of these years.

Think about it.

If *you* had been I and had wanted to set the record straight and could no longer approach the world in person with your story, how would *you* do it?

Through magic? Via incantations? With threats?

I considered them all.

Or would you find another way?

Starting things is always the most difficult part of life. I found that out, or rather I had that pointed out to me, many years ago. Once you have started upon your journey, the rest of the trip falls neatly into place. At least that has been my personal experience with life. So when I set about finding the right person to receive the truth, the real story of the life and times of Doc Holliday, and to deliver it to the masses, I knew in a heartbeat that everything would work out fine and dandy. I was my own daisy, and the feeling was grand.

"The medium is the message," a rather intellectually prominent and skillful crafter of the concept of effective communications had said years after I walked this ground. He was referring to how the process of disseminating information in the modern world unfolds. The medium is the message. It is a funny way of looking at things. I find it very humorous. During my day, it was just the other way around.

Nevertheless, I am always open to new ideas, to new discoveries and interpretations, and when I discovered a way to get my story out, the *real* story, well, I took it.

And I am telling it to you now, right here, as we sit and breathe. Forgive my play on words. I cannot tell you exactly how I am after all this time finally able to relay to you the reality of it all due to a matter of principle. I have allied myself with the forces of Good after having walked for so long amongst the armies of Evil. In a way, God has rewarded me for my perseverance, if you will call it that, for sticking to my beliefs as a Christian man and a southern gentleman. He has allied me with my own medium, by whom to carry my own message, and I cannot, will not, look a gift horse in the mouth.

This may be my one and only opportunity, and I have decided to take it. All whores be damned. Except, perhaps, for the one who struggles to keep up with me stride-for-stride at my side.

Verbum sapientis: A word to the wise.

A Man Called Doc

I knew Wyatt Earp on the day I was born. I do not point that out to you as a matter of boastful pride, but rather as a matter of simple fact.

Or I did not know Wyatt Earp, exactly, but I knew of a man such as he, a man such as I knew existed somewhere on the face of this earth, a man who I knew would grow to become someone whom I, myself, could grow to admire, a man such as I intended to befriend one day and, insomuch as possible, to emulate.

Now, I do understand—being a doctor of dentistry who has gone through medical school training and the sort—just how absurd it sounds to say that a newborn infant such as I could possibly have known what it is or who it is in particular that he intends someday to be like. I understand the absurdity of it all.

Yet, I persist. I knew from my earliest recollections, and—if I may interpolate, from far earlier than that—who I was at the moment of my birth and who I intended to become.

End of story.

Except for this: Imagine my surprise and my relative degree of disappointment when I learned sometime later in life that it simply could not be. Ever. *Ever.* My days were numbered, my life was limited, and my experiences were to be severely curtailed, unlike those of Wyatt Earp.

Of course, I never would have admitted that about myself during my own lifetime. But there is one thing I could not fail to admit: My days were marked no less poorly than a deck of fetid cards and, from the start, nearly never came to unfold at all.

My father was born Henry Burroughs Holliday on March 11, 1819, in Laurens County, South Carolina, to Robert Alexander and Rebecca (Burroughs) Holliday. He grew up in South Carolina, where all of the residents speak with an unnervingly disarming drawl, and when he completed school, he went to work as a pharmacist.

Sometime in 1831, my paternal grandfather resettled in Fayette County, Georgia, together with his wife Rebecca and six children—the first six of many more to come. My father by then had grown into a thin, wiry young man, tall and with chiseled good looks, who was well thought of by the local ladies.

When the Cherokee War broke out in 1838 over treaty rights that the Indians claimed had been granted to them in Texas and later denied by the U.S. government, my father joined the First Georgia Volunteers under Captain John D. Stills. Probably he did so as much out of a desire to experience the excitement that life so rarely offers one so young as to escape my grandfather's iron hand and growling demeanor and the overall daily drudgery of life on the farm.

In that respect, I can identify with the man: He was all right. He knew what the word *wanderlust* means, and he knew that the only way to satiate its otherwise insatiable demands was to face it head on.

So my father went off in search of recalcitrant savages, and he may have shot at one or two along the way. He was never too clear on that point. I am fairly confident, however, that the image of the blond-haired cavalryman, one boot on the ground and the other on the flanks of his downed horse, pistol drawn, steely eyes squinting, cartridges blazing as the savage Indians fell all around him, never actually transpired. In the end the entire war was more of a skirmish, and the expedition seemed no more exciting than a day at summer camp might appear today.

When the war that my father chased came to a rather ignominious end, with several pathetic-looking red men shackled and delivered to local authorities to haul off to jail and the rest of the tribes subdued, my father returned home just in time to learn of a new war on the horizon. This war, this *Mexican* War, unlike the one that had preceded it, must have seemed so much more exciting and with so much greater potential for action and intensity, because it actually involved another country, such as Mexico is. It gave my father opportunity anew to revel in the glory and spirit that national campaigns can bring to a man and that accompany such skirmishes not merely between two divergent groups of rat-eared human beings, but instead between two sovereign nations.

My father enlisted in "The Fannin Avengers" under the leadership of Harrison J. Sargent. The Avengers was a small group of volunteers that in time melded into a larger regiment commanded by Colonel Henry R. Jackson of Savannah. The group took its name in honor of the Georgia farm boys who had died with Colonel James Fannin at the Goliad Massacre during the Texas Revolution of 1836.

The Fannin Avengers were sent to Monterrey, Mexico, under the watch of none other than General Zachary Taylor and to Vera Cruz and Jalapa under General Winfield Scott, who was rightfully known as "Old Fuss and Feathers" for his insistence upon rigid military discipline, where my father was eventually discharged in the summer of 1847. Although still unmarried at the well seasoned age of twenty-eight, he returned to my grandparents' home in Georgia, carting along with him a ten-year-old orphan named Francisco Hidalgo, whom he planned to raise as his son.

Before long, my father met and began courting an attractive woman with naturally curly, dark hair and fiery dark eyes. Her name was Alice Jane McKey, a genuine southern beauty and fellow South Carolinian who was born on April 21, 1829, ten years my father's junior. The two entered into matrimonial bliss on January 8, 1849. Eleven months later, on December 3, they had a daughter, Martha Eleanora, who had become overnight the very pride of their lives. But the infant became sick during the wet spring of 1850 and died on June 12, possibly as a result of a diphtheria epidemic that had been sweeping the South. The death left my parents heartbroken.

The following year, on a typically steamy hot August day, my mother asked my father to ride to Fayetteville, a distance of twenty miles or so, to fetch his brother, John Stiles Holliday, who was a prominent physician of the day. My mother had been carrying me for nine months and sensed that labor was imminent. She had managed to maintain precious little faith in the score or so of local midwives who regularly tended to child-birthing matters, and for good reason. The mortality rates throughout the South were incredibly high, and my mother—after having seen my infant sister snatched from her bosom—was not about to risk the loss of another. For her good judgment and extraordinary perception, I shall always be grateful, although at times I wonder if such favor had not been misplaced.

Fortunately for both my mother and me, my father's brother, Uncle John—Dr. John S. Holliday—had matriculated from the highly regarded Georgia Medical College only seven years prior but had already made a name for himself as a well-respected surgeon throughout the region. My mother felt more comfortable in having my uncle oversee the delivery. Just in case.

So, on the eve of August 14, 1851, my father, his brother, and his sister-in-law Permelia arrived back at the Holliday household to deliver safely the newest resident of the Holliday clan. I understand that the delivery went without incident, a testimony to my uncle's medical prowess, I am sure. However, the aftermath of my birth left the good doctor concerned.

Upon examination, he found that I had emerged from the womb with a serious and potentially lethal birth defect: a cleft palate and partially cleft lip, today more commonly referred to as a harelip, a trait that would be no stranger to future generations of Hollidays. The cleft made suckling nearly impossible, which I assure you did not place me in good spirits, and my uncle instructed my mother on how to feed her newborn son with a spoon and an eyedropper, being careful not to cause me to choke or to breathe the food into my lungs, which could result in deadly pneumonia.

Before leaving for home, my uncle assured the family that surgery would correct the malformation. He suggested that I undergo an operation sometime after I had passed my first month's birthday. Although the surgery would have no effect on my inability to suck, it would allow me at least to eat and drink normally as I grew older and—just as importantly—leave only a minimal scar as a gentle reminder of what might have been.

My father, of course, informed my uncle that he would feel most gratified if John would perform the surgery, and the good doctor agreed. So, as I greeted my second month's natal day, the defects suffered during childbirth were repaired surgically by my uncle and a family cousin, the famed physician Crawford Long. Crawford was a graduate of Franklin College (now the University of Georgia) and had received his medical degree from the University of Pennsylvania in 1839. He was the first physician to use ether as an anesthetic in an operation that had required the removal of two small tumors from the neck of a young man by the name of James M. Venable. Or he was the first to do so successfully, at any rate.

My uncle had long been a great admirer of Crawford's surgical skills, particularly as they applied to knowing when and how to administer the anesthetic for various types of surgeries and childbirths. The two surgeons had consulted over yours truly, and Crawford accompanied my uncle to my parents' home on the date set for the reconstruction.

Luckily, the operation went well, and the repair left no permanent speech impediment, although I did require intensive speech therapy as I began to talk, a task that my mother took upon herself over the course of the next several years.

Although the operation had been skillfully performed, the slight scar left along my upper lip line was evidenced by the single genuine photograph that survives me, taken on the occasion of my graduation from dental school. But a slight scar, I can assure you, is far better than the possible alternatives, which I saw in other children less fortunate than I as I meandered my way through the early years of life.

In time, I grew into a healthy and, by all accounts, fairly beautiful baby boy with blue eyes and wavy blond hair, a set of pleasantries that would serve me well later in life. With considerable reason to give thanks, the entire Holliday family and related clans gathered at the First Presbyterian Church in Griffin to celebrate my belated christening on Sunday, March 21, 1852. Ironically, it was at the same church where my mother had been baptized only a year and a half earlier, on September 1, 1850. Although she had been born into a Methodist family, she had never enjoyed the rigors of formal religious training; so, at the age of twenty-three, in order to appease my father, she consented officially to join the exalted ranks of Presbyterianism. In a way, I always believed doing so suited her well: She had never liked to dance.

In the weeks that followed, my mother exhibited absolute devotion to the care of her young son. Following my uncle's advice, she was able to provide me with the nourishment that enabled me to live and thrive, although that often meant feeding me small amounts every two to three hours, a task that I cannot help but think exacted a serious toll on her physical and emotional well-being. As I grew, I developed a strong bond with the woman who proved to be my lifeline to the real world, and I recall rarely being far separated from her loving arms. Her determination must have rubbed off on me as we overcame the odds together, enabling me to gain steadily and most determinedly in weight and strength.

As the years passed, my mother showed herself to be a genteel, considerate, and refined southern woman who took great pleasure in providing for her young son's education. She spent most of her time helping me with my school work, teaching me to play the piano, and educating me in the unique manners and other pertinent refinements as befit a southern gentleman.

My father, on the other hand, turned out to be a good provider and a shrewd businessman who was, at various times in his life, a farmer, land speculator, store owner, public servant, and lawyer. Although somewhat high-strung and hot tempered, he was a good and a decent man, a true southern gentleman, and a loving husband and family man.

Six weeks prior to my baptism in 1852, my father had been commissioned as the first clerk of the Superior Court for Spalding County, quite a prestigious accomplishment. That position placed considerable demands on his time, but the family benefited politically, financially, and socially as a result. And the Hollidays—after years of sorrow and sadness following the death of my older sister—finally seemed to have everything going their way.

My Aunt Permelia, who had borne two young sons of her own, enjoyed spending as much time as possible with us. As a result, I grew especially close to my cousin. Robert, two years old to my one, proved to be impish and lively, always exploring, searching for frogs and toads and turtles and all manner of other living things and becoming extraordinarily exuberant with every new discovery. He also proved to be a good counterbalance for me, as I was more shy, quiet, and reflective in general, having been heavily sheltered by my mother because of my older sister's death and my own physical malady.

We spent most of our days together playing outdoors, which I particularly enjoyed. How I loved the sunlight and the fresh air. Frequently our mothers would pack together a picnic lunch and take us to nearby Cabin Creek in Griffin, and we would run and play and eat beneath the shade of the large cottonwoods growing alongside the water's edge. We would run around in the sunshine and chase the dogs, sometimes for hours on end, and then run wildly as the dogs turned to chase us, all the while our mothers chattering and tending to their needlework.

But when the playing was over and we returned home, my father was always there to make certain that his son recognized the realities of life, which in his eyes consisted of more than happenstance and good times. He had made his intent for me well known from as early as I can recall: Young John Henry Holliday would be endowed with all of the natural inheritance, the innate intelligence, and the endearing charms of a true Son of the South.

But not, I might add, if *I* had anything to say about it.

War!

GEORGIA ORDINANCE OF SECESSION

January 19, 1861

We the people of the State of Georgia in Convention assembled do declare and ordain and it is hereby declared and ordained that the ordinance adopted by the State of Georgia in convention on the 2nd day of January, in the year of our Lord seventeen hundred and eighty-eight, whereby the constitution of the United States of America was assented to, ratified and adopted, and also all acts and parts of acts of the general assembly of this State, ratifying and adopting amendments to said constitution, are hereby repealed, rescinded and abrogated.

We do further declare and ordain that the union now existing between the State of Georgia and other States under the name of the United States of America is hereby dissolved, and that the State of Georgia is in full possession and exercise of all those rights of sovereignty which belong and appertain to a free and independent State."

—*Georgia State Legislature, 1861*

We all cheered. We sang. We cried tears of great hope and joy. Across the sprawling length and width of the great state of Georgia, we rejoiced. Men and women and children to a one. We could not have been happier.

Perhaps not everyone understood the particulars of the rationale behind the concept of secession, but we definitely understood that it was a liberating experience, that it was freeing the South from the oppression of a centralized government that was leaning increasingly toward the industrialized North, toward its own self-interests and away from those of our beloved Georgians.

We also recognized the role that slavery had played in bringing the nation to the tipping point, of course. From a moral point of view, slavery may have been wrong. I will grant you that. But from a practical and a historical point of view, few people I knew could see much ill will in it.

I had personally grown up with slaves nearby me at all times, and never did they seem to be mistreated or violated by any stretch of the imagination. All the slaves I knew were happy to be where they were, happy to have a family and a house to call home and a roof over their heads and plenty to eat and someone to care about their welfare. They were not as well educated as the finest exemplars of the white ethnic majority, I must admit, and their education and intellect suited whatever jobs they could demonstrate that they could accomplish with any degree of proficiency. Some worked as butlers and housekeepers and maids while others toiled away as cotton strippers, field hands, gardeners, and livery attendants.

It is true that they did not get paid in currency of the realm, but they did get paid and, in some cases, quite generously for the services they were asked to provide. So when the federal government sought to keep new states from entering the Union as slave states—that is, states whose laws allowed for the buying, selling, trading, and keeping of slaves—we in the South were understandably distressed but not overly so and certainly not to the point of pressing for secession.

No, it was not the slavery issue at all that drove my beloved Georgia into bidding the United States Union goodbye; it was the intolerance by the North for the produce, labor, sweat, and tears provided by the South. All those northern Yankee homes and those northern Yankee factories could not have survived for three months without the food and produce and cotton and tobacco and cane that our southern states were expected to generate and to ship north for northerners' consumption. Not for three months. Yet, when the taxes were enacted and the constituents ordered to pay them, they were paid mostly by the southern states in order to provide for more factories and more railroads and more machinations divined by Washington to keep the North rolling in wealth and the South a poor second cousin.

When it became clear sometime earlier that nothing was going to change of benefit to the South without at first being of greater advantage to the North, the sound of the secessionist's bell tolling in the distance raised the rancor in our blood and set our hearts to beating faster. We saw secession as liberation from an oppressive government, and we responded to the mantra of southern rights with undeniable fervor.

And if the new Union government headed by the newly elected occupant of the White House, a Mr. A. Lincoln, hoped to entice the South to give up its notions of autonomy and return to the fold of Yankee protectionism by force, well, we southerners had learned a little something about how to fight over the years, and we knew more than a little about how to win. When it became clear after a Yankee attack on the South at Fort Sumter that there was no turning back, it became equally clear that our boys were itching to enlist, aching to put on a uniform to defend their newly liberated lands, the Southern Confederacy of America, and to fight for their homes and their families.

It would not take long. Everyone in the South truly believed that. When war proved to be inevitable, former senator Robert Toombs, who had just been named secretary of state of the Confederacy, addressed a crowd at the capital city of Milledgeville. He told a group of cheering Georgian recruits that they would be home within six months. Any good southern boy could whip six pasty-faced Yankee clerks, he reminded them. "Why," he proclaimed, "we could lick the Yankees with cornstalks!"

That was the feeling at the time for us Georgians. We did not go to the Yankees and ask for a fight, but by God we were not going to back away from one either. Let the Yankees come onto our lands and invade our homes and test our honor and try our mettle and see what would happen. We had no doubt that we were equal to the task of protecting all we had built up, all we had lived for these past hundred years. What our boys may have lacked in training and understanding of what lay ahead, they would more than make up for in confidence, determination, and loyalty. We never once thought that the South might actually lose. I sat around many a family gathering and listened to my uncles and my father and everyone else speak about enlisting in the war and serving their country, and I never once heard the mention of failure. The mere notion was anathema to them, as it was, I am certain, to the rest of the South.

Even our small Georgia town of Griffin shared in the excitement that precedes war. The mobilization of the enlistment camps and the pomp and circumstance that surrounded the signing of men young and old into the service certainly stirred my own furtive imagination. By the time Georgia had seceded from the Union, I was a half-grown boy of ten. I remember looking out the door or standing on the porch, waving, as the troops moved in and out of town, down the road, toward the rail yards, and I sometimes sneaked down to the station to catch a glimpse of them dressed in their silver finery, laughing and cheering and sometimes squeezing pretty women and kissing them and sometimes sitting pensively off alone somewhere, staring at their boots and wondering, I supposed even at that young age, what would happen to them next.

Camp Wilder had been converted into a training center for Georgia soldiers at Griffin, and Henry Holliday saw clearly enough that, if Georgia was to contribute finely turned fighting machines to the war effort, he would need to contribute 136 acres of his 147-acre farm for the establishment of such a facility. He sold the land to the government for a modest price. Georgia governor Joseph E. Brown wrote to Alexander H. Stephens, Georgia's former moderate congressman and the new vice president of the Confederacy, that two regiments had gone into training "at Camp Stephens, near Griffin, which I had called in honor of yourself."

War fever had struck at our very doorstep, and I was completely taken with it all. How could I not be?

I literally burst with pride as my family hero and favorite uncle, Thomas Sylvester McKey, who was at the time barely twenty-one, donned the uniform of the Fifth Georgia Vols and set off to see service. But for the fact that he had boosted me high above his head and boomed out in an uncharacteristically loud voice about how he was going to help the South "whup" those damned Yanks, I might have felt sad at seeing him off. But my Uncle Tom was not that kind of man. There was no sadness allowed when he walked into a room, and there was none proffered.

Soon thereafter, the other men of the Holliday and McKey clans followed in Thomas's footsteps: my uncles Robert Kennedy Holliday, John Stiles Holliday, James Taylor McKey, and William Harrison McKey, along with several of my cousins and, in turn, Francisco Hidalgo. My adopted brother was as anxious as anyone to serve his new homeland, as well as his family; and I suspect he also wanted to make our father proud. Who could blame him?

To a man, the family enlistees looked like a bunch of swells duded out in the secesh-gray uniforms of the Confederacy, all freshly laundered and starched. I found it of little surprise that the womenfolk gathered around them like bees around a hive full of honey as they prepared to march off on their great adventure. Even my cousin George, only five years my senior, was already enrolled at Georgia Military Institute in Marietta, dreaming of the day he, too, might be called upon to defend his beloved Georgia from the invading hoards of the North.

For a ten-year-old boy filled with love and admiration for the men in his life, it was a time of great joy and laughter, but also of deep sorrow and tears. War is hell, no matter how you look upon it, no matter whence it comes or during what epoch it decides to visit. But to a young Georgia boy who secretly wished that he, too, could march off with the others to prove his bravery and return with a chest full of ribbons and medals and citations, it was a time of intense excitement. And then, before we had an opportunity even to stop to think much more about it, they were gone.

My father had been the last of the Hollidays to go. He had bought another 278 acres south of the land he already owned and made provisions for his family as best he could. Finally, on September 2, 1861, Henry Burroughs Holliday was commissioned a major in the Twenty-seventh Georgia Infantry. On October 31 he followed the footsteps of my other kinfolk off to Virginia, where he served as quartermaster officer, arriving in time for the first battle of Manassas. He left our slave Sophie to watch over my mother and me and the others to grow the crops necessary to sustain us. He placed my mother in charge—as had other husbands in other southern households—of all family affairs and business.

That was the first time I realized that watching the men go off to battle in a faraway place was not all pomp and circumstance. It struck me suddenly that my father's absence was going to be a hardship on everyone he left behind. He was the backbone of the family, its solid core, and now he was gone. Worse, nobody knew for sure when he would return.

The excitement that had existed as the Hollidays and McKeys left to fill the ranks of the Confederate forces quickly faded into anxiousness. We daily found ourselves desperate to learn news about the war. Which battles had been fought, who had been involved in the skirmishes, how many men had been injured, how many killed?

But not even the daily news was much help on matters that truly concerned us: Where was Henry Burroughs Holliday, and how was he faring? Was he still high of spirits and well of health? And what of my cousins and adopted brother? What of my favorite uncle and the others? Not knowing was the worst part about staying behind, by far.

Our most reliable information often came in the form of gossip passed from one southern plantation to another. Someone would receive a letter from someone at the front, and news of it would spread throughout the South, fueled no doubt by the speculation of the newspapers and flyers printed and disseminated throughout Georgia. Occasionally we would glean bits and pieces from people we actually knew, friends and neighbors, but more often than not, the information passed along to us was of far too general a nature to satisfy our curiosities, which grew greater with each passing day.

Adding to my own frustrations as a young boy was the fact that I found myself in the middle of a household of women who—as women everywhere are predisposed to do—spread much more gossip than fact. In so doing they managed to cast a net about me, clinging to me tenaciously, my mother and my aunts especially, as I was one of the few males of the family still too young to don a uniform or enroll in the academy.

So I found myself over the period of the next few months in a precarious situation for a growing young man of indomitable will and spirit, if not actual bravado. At precisely that time before puberty sets in when gentlemen are supposed to take up with their sons and teach them the manly arts of refinement, my father not only was conspicuously absent—and in his stead none others available to step forward to fill his shoes—but also I was immersed in feminine chicanery, forced to endure the spying and the sighing, the sobbing and the crying, and all other manner of female behavior that came with it. Instead of beginning my apprenticeship into life as a young man, as all southern boys my age were expected to do, I had begun to learn how to cackle. I swear to God, if it had lasted another twelve months, I would have grown bosoms and taken up needlepoint.

In self-defense I set out on my own path to learn those skills and mannerisms that are so critical to the genteel way of the Gentleman of the South. If no one else were available to fill my father's shoes, well, by God, I would take the burden upon myself.

It turned out to be an uneasy task.

Having spent a good deal of my early childhood recovering from an acute abnormality and learning how to speak at my mother's dear hands, I had acquired only the most basic rudiments of the arts of hunting, fishing, wrestling, pistol shooting, and horsemanship. Oh, I could ride, and I could drop a baited hook into the stream, and I could do all sorts of things such as those; I simply could not do them well enough for a boy my age.

Gradually I came to the disposition that opportunities for learning lay all around the town of Griffin, extending well beyond the lily-white walls that the Holliday-McKey womenfolk had erected around me. And I leapt upon every opportunity I encountered to partake of them, let me assure you. I skulked my way through the woods and imagined myself keeper of the safety of home and hearth. I fought off imaginary Yankees and ruthless cutthroats who preyed mercilessly upon those less skilled than I. I stole down to the very edge of Camp Stephens, where I watched the recruits drill and train, and learned from them how to prepare for war. I imposed myself brazenly upon any adult males I could find—young or old—gathered around the back room of the general store or in the town's barber shop or even right outside the local saloon, asking them precocious questions and hanging upon their every word.

Or I would feign, when someone spoke, not to listen. I would pretend to be preoccupied, too much so to pay any attention to what was being bantered about, but in reality I would listen to every word, and I would think upon every single thing that I heard.

On rare occasion we would get news of the war whenever my uncle, John Stiles, paid us one of his increasingly rare visits. Uncle John was the only man in the family to remain near to home. As a physician in good standing, he had been made medical officer of Company E, the Fayette Dragoons, Second Georgia Cavalry, part of Georgia's home guard. He was in charge, to a great degree, of maintaining the health and the welfare of the recruits bivouacked in Griffin, and although his duties as such and in practicing medicine among the general populace preoccupied an inordinate amount of his time, he occasionally found the opportunity to come back to visit with us, with his brother's family, and to make whatever enquiries he could pertaining to our own health and well-being.

It was on those occasions, however fleeting, that I would be reunited with my cousin Robert; and we would exchange information about what we had discovered relative to growing up, to becoming a man, and occasionally to other things less properly shared here—as well as about war and death and valor and the fairer gender and all sorts of things that accompany the unfolding of the human drama.

We would talk, too, about my father. Robert had an inordinate amount of love and respect for Henry Holliday, much the way I had for Robert's father, Uncle John. Sometimes, however, I would listen to him talking about what a great and honorable man my father was and how lucky I was to be his son, and something would turn upside down inside my skull. *What on earth is he talking about?* I would ask myself.

Of course, my father was an honorable man. But he had also gone off to pursue the vagaries of war, leaving me behind to suffer the enduring agony of my own mother's upbringing and that of my surrogate family. That in itself would not have been so bad had he not done so at the precise moment when nature and the traditions of the South determined that I should be taken under wing and *properly* educated.

I longed to know how to do such things as face down a man in a duel, stand up for womanhood in my chivalry, slaughter a charging boar, and place food on the table in times of great adversity. I dreamed of walking the line between scoundrel and paragon, coming down on the right side every time. I fantasized about finding a woman of my own and making her fall in love with me, making her want to marry me some day so that we would have children of our own and I could teach them—the boys, of course—in the ways of the true southern gentleman. And when we would walk along the streets of downtown Griffin in the early evening before the sun went down, people would smile and doff their hats to me and tell me what a lovely day it was and what a wonderful family I had and how fortunate everyone was to have enjoyed our acquaintance.

Those are a great many things for a prepubescent boy of ten going on eleven to think about and to reflect upon, and I discovered that, the more time that passed, the more I found myself rebelling against the influence of the women in my life, the more I found myself resenting my father's prolonged absence—and to a lesser degree the other Holliday and McKey men of the family as well—and the more I resented the length of time between visits from my Uncle John and Robert.

I began developing a—oh, what is it?—a certain brashness about me, and I embarked upon a period of rebellion that, while not totally uncommon among young boys my age, was nevertheless totally unacceptable. I was acting out against the very family that loved me most, not the least of which included my own mother. I was becoming a difficult child when the members of my family needed me most to be compliant and eager to help. I even fantasized about running away, escaping the very backbone of our family, in order to join the Confederacy in its noble rage against the North.

I see now how foolish I had been and I hope that my ascribing it to the folly of youth is sufficient excuse. The women of the South, especially those of a similar class and stature to my mother's, have proven themselves time and again to be strong and flexible, bending and rigid, and always imbued with social elegance and good moral fiber. They expect to be treated properly at all times, and more than expect, they *demand* it of their men and of society in general.

That is not to say that southern women are spoiled or pampered. Just the opposite. Women of my mother's distinction bore many sacrifices, and they did so with a sense of stoic pride. The tradition of having been brought up in gentility marked them with a sense of manners, abstinence, and social restraint rarely seen today. They enjoyed the honor of knowing they were loyal in marriage, unblemished in society, and proud of their men, particularly of those men who had marched off to war.

Southern women experienced the desperate loneliness of their husbands' prolonged absences with scant complaint. Even when those absences placed an extraordinary burden upon them—such as in the case of raising one John Henry Holliday—they rarely balked and never complained. Of their daughters, they were adamant that they be raised to reflect the social graces all too well known to fine young women in every traditional southern Christian sense of the word. Of their sons, they were supportive of their husbands' attempts by whatever means available to them to turn them from unrefined alley urchins into young southern gentlemen of gentility and honor.

This task, in the absence of a suitable man in my own life, fell by default upon the shoulders of my mother and the other women of the Holliday household. It was they who would have to teach John Henry to be a gentleman—or at least make some minor inroads into his introductions.

So there for me was my personal quagmire. Young boys of the South are encouraged to fight and scrap and do whatever myriad things that differentiate young boys from young girls. Yet, just as I began my struggle to find my role as a young gentleman in southern Christian society, I was being reigned in by the only people in my family I had left to whom I could turn for help and knowledge and support. My mother did her best to ameliorate the chidings of her sisters and sisters-in-law with the knowledge of her role and obligation as a lady of infinite refinement.

But it was I who was still caught in the middle.

I might never have grown past that year—that tumultuous, contentious, and most confusing of years—but for something that suddenly awakened in me a keener interest in what was going on in the real world around me.

It happened one morning, when I rose and prepared myself for school. After climbing into my breeches and clean shirt, slipping into my shoes, running a brush through my hair, and wiping my teeth free of grunge in a clean white linen rag by the wash basin, I went into the kitchen to greet my mother, who would be instructing our servant on what to prepare and how best to prepare it. Instead, I found our Sophie alone. When I inquired of her as to my mother's whereabouts, she told me that Miss Alice Jane was under the weather and unable to get out of bed this morning. Most likely it would pass.

I thought about going into her room to check on her and decided instead to move forward with my plans for the day.

Later, several weeks after, she fell more seriously ill with what my uncle had finally diagnosed as a chronic pulmonary disorder, something he called consumption.

At the time few people realized what consumption was, although I would not for long be among them. It was a common illness and one from which many people died. It was the cancer of our age, tuberculosis, the dreaded lung disease, accounting for up to 20 percent of all deaths in our great nation.

Unfortunately, doctors were sadly ill prepared to diagnose or prescribe for tubercular patients. They believed the disease to be non-contagious, a belief that would later cost me dearly. Instead, it was something that people picked up from somewhere, and it seemed to run in families, like big ears and freckles.

Treatment varied depending upon the gender of the infected person. Women were encouraged to remain within the home and pursue their domestic responsibilities as much as possible, maintaining a cheerful and upbeat demeanor for the benefit of husband and children alike. And so came Uncle John's prescription.

Surprisingly, the malady's victims often were viewed with sympathy and admiration. The hideous physical symptoms of consumption were thought to be an ennobling purger of the basest qualities of humanity and a distiller of the loftier ones. Perhaps because of their upbringing, women in particular wore the banner well, complaining little to outsiders and family and expecting less in return for their pain and suffering. And often receiving it.

In the case of my mother, I felt confident that she would not become a statistic. She was far too noble a woman to reach that end. A pious person of gentle soul who bore no malice toward anyone, she was as pure and pristine as the early morning sun over the Georgia hillside. If ever a woman would recoup from the disease, Alice Jane Holliday was she.

But apparently somebody forgot to tell that to the disease, which continued to plague her, despite my uncle's best efforts, over the next several months. While I grew to blame my father for my mother's illness—having left her with too much to do, too much to care for—I knew that blame alone would not win the day. I knew that I had to step up and see to her mending—as she had done for me years earlier in my life. I was not quite sure how best to accomplish so staggering a task in its complexity, but with help from almighty God, I was determined to learn.

Within a matter of hours, I had transformed myself from an insecure, rebellious, searching young wretch of a boy into the man of the house. I did so in more than mere name. I suddenly found myself the only living Holliday male overseeing hundreds of acres of land, half a dozen slaves, and an ailing mother.

And so I made a vow. It would be I—John Henry Holliday—who would save my mother from the ravages of a disease that had claimed so many others so indiscriminately before her. It would be *I* who would save her very life.

And my father be *damned*.

The End of Innocence

L ong before I met Wyatt Earp, long before I was old enough in effect to meet practically anyone, I was already upset and angered and seething. Oh, do not take me the wrong way. I tried not to show it. I tried my best to hold it in, for that is the nature of a southern Christian gentleman. I tried, and I succeeded. For much of the time.

It was summer 1862; and, although the War between the States was destined to rage on for another three years, for some of the men of the Holliday and McKey families, the war was just about over.

Thankfully, none of the men of my family suffered the ultimate indignation of the injustices of war during the conflagration that was to last ultimately for four years. But my father, Henry, did not fare so well. He had been struck not by a musket ball, but instead by a severe case of "chronic diarrhea and general disability" that kept him out of battle. The illness that plagued him became so virulent that he finally was forced to resign his commission in the summer of 1862, after which he was discharged on August 24 and set upon his mount headed for home.

Our family, of course, was ecstatic. My mother, whom I thought to be in less than the best of health despite the ministrations of my esteemed uncle and his enthusiastic, if young, nephew, was particularly overjoyed. At last her strength, her hope, her joy, her beloved husband, was coming home, coming home to pick up where he left off on that fateful day one year hence when he marched off to join in the war.

But the home my father returned to was quite different than the one he had left to go and fight for the Confederacy. Oh, I don't mean different in the sense that Tara was different after the war had visited the plantation in *Gone With the Wind.* I mean somehow *otherwise* different.

Oh, yes. I see what is on your mind, and I will address the matter straight away. I *can* read, you understand. I can see and I can hear and I can understand and even to some degree know what people are thinking about, some more than others. Why that is I do not know.

In the long and short of it, it's this: If it happened, I know about it.

So I have been able to compare our Georgia home with those fictional domiciles of the past and say that it did fare better than they. Nevertheless, the ravages of war had taken a heavy toll upon our community, our state, and much of the South. Commerce was nearly nonexistent. Goods were scarce and expensive, when you could find them at all. The fields were neglected, and food crops were in extremely short supply.

Imagine going into a dry-goods store and finding the shelves bare, except perhaps for a few cans of beans, a five-pound sack of sugar, and some tobacco. How would *you* have gotten along?

And then there was the question of the Negro slave. Had Lincoln freed him or not? There was rampant rumor everywhere that he had. Either that or he was going to do so in the near future. We could not, in the South, pause to reflect upon how one man sitting in a large mansion in Washington, D.C., could visit so much power upon his office as to be able to banish an entire lifestyle with the stroke of a quill. Nevertheless, word had gotten out that slavery had ended, and many slaves had abandoned their masters' plantations. Others had left to show their support for the Confederacy, having believed that the notion their white masters had placed in their heads about the North trying to end the southern way of life—for better or for worse—through the use of armed force was true.

Others, still, had heard that the North was accepting colored men of an appropriate age into the armed services, where they would receive training, food, clothes, and everything else they could possibly desire, including shoes for their feet and balls and powder for their newly government-issued rifles, after which their discharge from military service would leave them free men.

So this is the Georgia to which my father returned, only to find his wife bedridden and uncertain what to do about her failing health. To make matters worse, a few months later saw my grandfather, Robert, the Holliday family patriarch and one of the wisest men I have ever known, pass on in Fayetteville.

As the eldest son, my father was required to leave our home yet again and travel to the town to oversee the funeral arrangements and the distribution of my grandfather's estate, which he eventually divided equally among his siblings. With that barely settled, we received more bad news. The Confederacy had suffered a major defeat that fall at Gettysburg, followed by the fall of Vicksburg to the Union Army in July of the following year. It became clear to my father that the South was not faring well at all. What wasn't so clear was what exactly would happen next.

From the Front, news of the war continued to be bad. Although the Johnnies fought bravely to a man and pulled from the fires of defeat an occasional wretched victory, the major battles were falling the other way. On September 19–20, 1863, the opposing armies met at Chickamauga in northern Georgia just south of the Tennessee line, where Lieutenant James Longstreet's forces, under General Braxton Bragg's command, broke through, driving two Union corps off the field and scattering a large number of General Rosecrans's forces into full retreat. Union General George Thomas, the "Rock of Chickamauga," stood firm on the right, the only thing between the Army of the Potomac and a Confederate route.

Pleased with the fighting there, President Jefferson Davis left Bragg in command, despite protests from his own officers. It was one of the greatest mistakes of Jeff Davis's short but distinguished career, and it would cost the South dearly.

The North sent General Ulysses S. Grant, now commander in chief of the Army of the West, to turn the tide of battle at Chickamauga. On November 23, 1863, following a Union rout at Lookout Mountain, Grant set his eyes upon Bragg's forces, still occupying the high ground of Missionary Ridge. Two days later Union troops, in a wild display of unbridled bravado rarely exhibited north of the Mason-Dixon line, charged the Confederate position, panicking the Johnnies and sending them running for their very lives. It was, in the words of one Southern official, an "incalculable disaster."

The doorway into Georgia had been jarred open.

With the Confederate forces under General Johnston digging in at Dalton, not far from the Chickamauga battlefield, and Union forces plus generals Grant and William Tecumseh Sherman eyeing a coming confrontation, my father decided it was time to clear his family out of the line of fire. He knew that the Union's main target would be the railroad hub at Atlanta; so he began selling property in Spalding County to raise money for the move.

Between August 1863 and April 1864, Major, by which name my father was increasingly invested, raised nearly $24,000 in Confederate currency from the sale of his real estate holdings in Griffin and in Spalding County and set his sights on moving the family to the southern Georgia town of Valdosta.

Valdosta was about as far away from the war as a person could get and still be glued to this earth. Near the end of the rail line and ringed by undeveloped pine forests and wire grass, it was a dismal place. Once anticipated to be a thriving metropolis, it fell into disrepair when the Atlanta and Gulf Railroad bypassed nearby Troupville, named after former governor George M. Troup, by several miles. Not wanting to miss out on the economic boom the railroad promised to bring to town, most of the townspeople picked up and moved their businesses from Troupville to the tracks, where the new town was named after the former governor's mansion, Val d'Aosta, later shortened to Valdosta.

This newly sprouted metropolis was still "cropping up out from the woods" when the war began, according to the *South Georgia Times*.

Whatever promises the railroad gave for the financial success of the town were quickly pulled back by the war, as buildings stood half-completed and the town itself was all but abandoned. A Union Army blockade and two years of failed crops nearly ended Valdosta altogether. Even God seemed to have abandoned the place: When my father first arrived, he found both the Methodist and the Baptist churches in rubble, having blown to the ground in a fierce storm.

Still, Henry Holliday was a shrewd businessman, and he knew that the war was playing out far from Valdosta soil. So, on February 9, 1864, he purchased 2,450 acres from the estate of James D. Shanks on Cat Creek northeast of the town for $31,500 in Confederate money. He returned to Griffin, settled our family affairs, closed up the house, and gathered family and slaves, along with whatever personal items we could carry, for the trip to our new home.

So it was that, by April 1864, I found myself a refugee in a strange land. Not quite turned 13, I felt an overwhelming sense of abandonment, although I could not at the time attribute to the feeling any rationale. In retrospect, I imagine the sparseness of the area and the lack of the red Georgia clay that I had grown up with in my childhood added to my forlornness.

My father, on the other hand, seemed to revel in the challenges facing him. He recognized almost from the beginning the potential for agriculture in the rich black loamy soil of the area. He must have salivated at the thought of raising cotton, buying more slaves, and making a fortune from the acreage he had recently purchased with money that would soon be worth less than the paper upon which it had been printed.

News of the war reached Valdosta only sporadically, as we seemed to have been deposited at the very apex of hell. Eventually, we learned of General Sherman's intent to march his troops through Atlanta while laying waste to the city. True enough, on August 30, 1864, Hood's troops were badly mauled at Jonesboro, and the following day Sherman hit the Confederacy hard again. Hood evacuated Atlanta on September 1, destroying everything of military value in the process, and on September 2 Sherman wired Washington, "Atlanta is ours, and fairly won." Each day thereafter brought us scant more news—some of it occasionally even accurate.

On September 15 my father, who was in Macon attending to business at the time, wrote to Mollie, my Uncle Robert's wife, that he would be back in the area within a week and that he wanted to take her home with him for safety's sake. My uncle Robert wrote her, ". . . you don't know how glad I was to hear that you had left Jonesboro, for I was perfectly miserable thinking how you and our little children could live inside of the Yankee lines or even where our own army are, for there is not as much difference in them as there ought to be, but when I heard you had got away I was happy indeed."

My father unfortunately hadn't the time to return to retrieve her; but on another day early in October, while he was tying his horse to a hitching post near the Valdosta railroad station, he looked up to see his sister-in-law and her children standing on the platform. Absolutely stunned to find them there—apparently their note to Major had been a casualty of war—he quickly gathered them up, whisked them to the farm, and provided for them a home of their own in which to live. After the fall of Atlanta, Sherman wrote Grant that he could make a march to the sea "and make Georgia howl." Although we did not know at the time what that meant, we soon enough found out. On November 15, 1864, Sherman burned Atlanta to the ground and began his devastating and despicable march through the length and breadth of our beloved Georgia.

My cousins Mattie and Lucy had barely managed to escape from the city during the general evacuation, not yet realizing that Cousin George was part of the forces covering the withdrawal. The two girls joined the rest of the family on our farm in time for Christmas.

I remember being overjoyed at being reunited with my kin, and in the months that followed, Mattie and I grew exceedingly close. A rambunctious and, at times, rebellious young man, I was discovering the joys and dogged determination of puberty, and I confess an unholy alliance with my thoughts over the young woman, who was older than

I and charming in all ways along the lines of traditional southern womanhood—charming and vexing and flirtatious. I found her to be a bewitching aberration amongst the hard realities of life by which I was surrounded.

In fact, my feelings toward the girl were such that I might have pursued more than I had, given the fact that marriages between first cousins in those days—especially amongst southerners—were not that uncommon. The local land barons and plantation owners found such civil unions to be an efficient means of expanding their territorial and real property holdings. I must say I had entertained just such a notion myself on more than one occasion, as the two of us walked hand in hand along the lane down toward the river or took a turn or two in the buggy around town.

My mother by that time had become virtually an invalid despite every possible thing we could think of to help her get well; and my father, by his very nature, grew distant and understandably preoccupied with providing for a house full of family. Mattie made things bearable for me, and I returned the favor by throwing my attentions at her shamelessly, although at the time I was sure that no one felt I was being any more attentive and loving than a cousin should attempt to be during those most trying of moments.

But, alas, my uncle and aunt were Catholics, and Canonical law of the Holy Roman Catholic Church strictly forbade the marrying of first cousins, and possibly third and fourth as well—I am only guessing at the latter. Thus I knew that Mattie and I—barring some unforeseeable circumstance, such as my cousin denouncing the church and becoming a Protestant or a Presbyterian or even, God forbid, a Methodist— would always know a love of unspoken and unrequited consumption. We would never be more than loving, caring, doting cousins.

More the shame.

In many ways, my father, always the practical man that he was, was shrewder and more perceptive than many, and while he no doubt noticed the strength of the emotional bonds between my cousin and me, he nevertheless also saw the barriers to any further developments.

He could have stepped in and put his foot down, but he knew instinctively that he needed not do so. Just as he foresaw the outcome of that relationship, he foresaw the outcome of the war and, knowing that Confederate currency would soon be worthless, reached out to purchase an additional thousand acres of land for $3,150 in Confederate funds from the Shanks' estate in 1865. Then he sat back to await the end of the war and the wrath of Old Man Shanks.

It was not until nearly a month following the surrender of General Lee at Appomattox in April 1865 that we learned of the treaty. Gradually, the remaining Hollidays and McKeys who had fought gallantly for the preservation of our homeland began funneling themselves home. As tough and uncertain as times were, our family had reason to rejoice. Every man to a one returned alive and well. Eventually, Robert took his family back to Jonesboro to begin the rebuilding process, even though everything he had owned had been destroyed. Other members of the Holliday family also returned to their homes in the area of my beloved childhood.

My father, along with several other family members, decided to stay in Valdosta and make it our permanent residence. Before long, I had enrolled in school once more, studying under a man named Professor Mathis, who held classes at the recently renovated Valdosta Institute. He was joined shortly thereafter by Samuel McWhir Varnedoe, who settled in Valdosta in November 1865. A tough but fair man, he gave his students ample opportunity to show off their newly acquired classical educations to proud parents and neighbors. We went on various outings as well, and in that rich coeducational environment, we were offered opportunities to improve our social skills. And, of course, to flirt with the girls.

Already well mannered and charming as the result of my mother's instruction and my grounding in a large, well-educated family, I learned quickly both in the classroom and in the social arena how to be popular with the opposite sex. I was considered a strong-minded, confident, and even cocky young man by our neighbors. In fact, everyone in our family enjoyed a position of admiration and social elegance, due to what particular reasons I might only guess. But I do know that my father—who had played many roles within the state's communities—was both admired and lauded. My mother, long suffering and never for want of a kind word, was given the respect and adulation to which she was entitled.

In short, life in Valdosta proved more tolerable than I had anticipated it to be.

And then everything ground to a halt.

On May 30, 1866, my father accepted an appointment as an agent for the Freedmen's Bureau. He was assigned the arduous task of integrating the blacks into the mostly white southern community. The appointment did not sit well with friends or neighbors, who feared and resented the blacks with their newly found freedoms and often confrontational attitudes that accompanied them. And it did not sit well with me. Believing as I did that the freedmen were a source of shame to the way of life we had lived for hundreds of years, the knowledge that my father would be working with them on a daily basis ate away at me like a weevil on a cotton bud.

I was not alone, as most of our friends and neighbors turned on him as well, denouncing him suddenly as a "worthless scalawag" and a "ruffian," an opportunist and a carpetbagger. In their minds my father had become synonymous with Yankee excesses, black-lovers, and carpetbaggers everywhere, and they denounced him as a "wicked spy," an "ignorant ass," and a "moral leper" throughout the years of his service. And those they saw to be his *good* points.

Sadly, as I reflect upon it today, I found it more and more difficult if not impossible to come to his defense. Little did I realize that things were only going to get worse.

Love, Death, Betrayal, Etc.

The Valdosta Watchman, *September 1866*

She was confined to her bed for a number of years, and was indeed a greater sufferer. She bore her afflictions with Christian fortitude. It has never fallen to my lot to know a more cheerful Christian. It was a great pleasure to visit her to see the triumph of religion over the ills of life.

She was deeply solicitous about the welfare of all she loved. She fully committed them into the hands of a merciful God with the full awareness that God would hear and answer her prayers, and that her instructions and Christian example would still speak.

She was deeply anxious about the faith of her only child. She had her faith written so her boy might know what his mother believed. She was for a time a member of the Presbyterian Church and never subscribing in heart to their article on election she determined to change her Church relation as she was not willing to die and leave on record for her boy that she subscribed to said faith. She therefore joined the M. E. Church whose doctrines she heartily accepted.

I visited her a few days before her death; she was calm, cheerful, joyful. She said to me that there was not a dimming veil between her and her God. She thus passed away from the Church militant to the Church triumphant, leaving her friends to mourn not as those who have no hope, knowing their loved one is not dead but sleepeth.

It happened—the inevitable—on September 16, 1866. As our minister spoke these eloquent words, I could scarce believe they were said over the smoldering embers of my eternally beloved mother.

She was not a saint; I understood that. She was not a martyr; I understood that as well. She was not and never could be all things to all people. To me, she was much more, and as I listened to the words, I felt as if some egregious wrong had been aggravated against her soul. It had been a mistake—God in his own fumbling way had somehow managed to get it wrong and errantly called his daughter prematurely to his side. How could it be otherwise? Why would he, in all his wisdom and glory, take so precious a woman and deliver her from her family's hands? How *could* he? How *dare* he! I half-expected her to appear beside me at the funeral, radiant and smiling as always—even through her darkest hours—and embrace me, pull me to her side, and hold me tight. "It's all right, my darling son. It was all one big mistake. But it's all right now."

But she did not appear at my side, which I took to be a sign that perhaps God had not made a mistake after all. Perhaps it was I who, in the ignorance and arrogance of youth, had made the mistake. Perhaps he, for some reason known only to himself, wanted her with him from that day forward.

I understand all too well about the shortness of life now, of course, having lived myself in the shadow of death for more than a decade. But to a fifteen-year-old boy already reeling from the indignities heaped upon himself and his family by his father's insensitivities within the community, it was a hardening blow.

The silence within our household that ensued following my mother's demise was unbearable. I had never known such a feeling.

Even the sound of her coughing late into the night, her gasping for air when there was none to be had, her wheezing and spitting up phlegm and blood had somehow grown to be comforting to me. As long as she was alive, I had hope. As long as she was here, I had hope. Now all was gone.

There was nothing left to do but to try to stumble forward. The coming year would be one of solitude and reflection for me. During that period of mourning, it would fall to me, the only son of Alice Jane McKey Holliday, to garb myself entirely in black for nine months, followed by a three-month period of wearing only gray. It was the proper thing to do. The same for my father, my innocent mother's one and only grieving husband. For the next twelve months, we would severely curtail our social activities in order to avoid any appearance of impropriety, any hint of the acceptance into our hearts of anything other than painful sorrow. That, I thought to myself, would be the easy part—living the life of the cloistered; for there was no happiness left within me.

And then, just when it seemed as if life could get no worse, the entire community exploded in a vociferous rage aimed only at us when, a mere three months following his wife's death and her internment in Sunset Hill Cemetery, Major married his neighbor's daughter, a twenty-three-year-old girl by the name of Rachel Martin. Reverend Ousley performed the ceremony—the same man who had revered my mother only weeks before. Although he had chosen to forgive my father's foregoing of the customary mourning period and bless this new alliance, the town did not. Major and his new bride had enjoyed no time for a courtship. Or had they? The tongues throughout Valdosta wagged, as they will in situations of this bend. Word reached me through my few friends and confederates that suspicions about my father and our neighbor had begun to surface. How long had they been carrying on? What had they been up to? And how could he—a onetime pillar of the community—defile his relationship with my mother so?

As great as the shock to the town had been, the insult I felt my father had dealt to the memory of my mother was insufferable. I was angry. I was incensed. Had I had the strength and the know-how, I would have killed him with my bare hands, had the opportunity presented itself to me. Instead, I would forevermore be unable to look upon my father again without feeling the pain and degradation that he had so errantly heaped upon the very soul of his one and only son.

I was not alone. My mother's family was also upset by my father's lack of respect for their dearly departed sister. The McKey brothers openly questioned whether or not my father had remained faithful to their sibling. I suspect that they already knew the answer.

Shortly after my father's December wedding to his new blushing bride, my Uncle Tom filed a lawsuit against his brother-in-law to recover his sister's property, which would customarily have been passed down to the surviving marital partner. The most important piece of property involved was the Iron Front Building in downtown Griffin, Georgia.

Following a bitterly contested legal battle, the presiding judge eventually divided the building into two parts, awarding half to the McKey family and the other half to Major in legal guardianship of his son. A partition was erected down the center of the building, and the owners took their respective possessions.

Although the judge's decision had settled the legal issues, the magistrate in all his wisdom could do nothing to mend the fences that had been broken down between the two families. I doubt that the McKeys ever forgave my father for his insensibilities.

In time, the town went on to reel from other scandals, as all towns do, and the memory of my father's dalliance grew cold. But it did not cool within me. I could never forgive his betrayal. My feelings were only intensified by his decision to leave our farm at Cat Creek and move his family into a home on Savannah Avenue owned by his new in-laws.

Living in town was anathema to me. Living in town beneath the constant reminder of what my father had done—and not understanding how or why he could possibly have done so—was even worse.

At school that year I lost much of the amiability for which I had developed a reputation. I grew solitary and quarrelsome. While fine southern boys were expected to experiment with fighting, gambling, swearing, drinking, and whoring—all activities that tested the schoolboy's mettle amongst his peers—I chose instead to become aggressive to the point of vindictiveness.

On one occasion, following a quarrel with one of my classmates, I was challenged to a duel with pistols. I gladly accepted.

The two of us were to meet on the field of honor, each with our seconds. A box containing two pistols filled with powder but not balls was laid before us, and I was given my choice. I replied instead that I would use my own pistol, and I remarked that it was well loaded with lead.

My Uncle Tom McKey, writing about the incident years later, got it mostly right when he said that my opponent and our seconds "were very much disconcerted over this statement by young Holliday. It was supposed to have been a 'mock' duel and here was Holliday with a loaded pistol meaning business! They urged him to use one of the powder-loaded pistols, but to no avail. He had his own gun and that was the one he was going to use in this affair.

"Seeing that they could not persuade Holliday to use one of the harmless guns, the seconds and his opponent had to explain to him that the duel was a kind of joke. But John was satisfied that 'the joke wasn't on him.' There was no duel, and an amicable settlement was made between the two young men."

I don't know to this day if I would actually have gone through with the duel, although I suspect that I might have. If for no other reason than to express to my father my anger over those things that I could not discuss with him, could not ask of him outright for fear of the answers, I might have.

That is where I found my mind during those tumultuous times—on the edge of a daily unfolding melodrama filled with disaster. Somehow I managed to muddle through those next trying years, until in 1869, with my formal education nearly completed, I took a job working at the Valdosta station for the Atlantic & Gulf Railroad. In April of that year, William and Tom McKey bought some land in nearby Troupville, and I found myself spending more time with my favorite uncle. I do believe my latching onto him as a surrogate father may have saved me from a life of hate and disdain. It may even have saved my very existence, worthless as it seemed at the time.

But that was not the turning point in my life. As important as my relationship with my uncle had become to me, there was an even more critical one that lay right around the corner. And for better or for worse, it would form the cornerstone of my existence for the rest of my days on earth.

The Doctor Is In

I might never have taken the next step in my life's journey had it not been for a minor incident involving a group of colored boys down by the watering hole on the Withlacoochee River where we used to go to swim—often sans clothing. On this particular occasion, when a group of us arrived, we found several young Negroes who had beaten us to the spot and, since this was our day and our swimming hole, we told them to pick up their belongings and leave. Just like that.

And they told us that they would not, and that if we didn't like them there, then we could go find another spot in which to do our swimming, for they were not about leaving. Just like that.

I turned to my friends, who by now had begun to winnow away from the confrontation, and glanced at my Uncle Tom, who was still holding his ground. Emboldened and anxious to display my prowess in the presence of my very favorite member of the family, I pulled from my belongings a pistol and proceeded to fire several shots over their heads.

They left.

The following day, I was on my way by horseback to Atlanta in order to spend some "reflective time" with another of my uncles, Robert Kennedy Holliday. Although my father had never said so, I always suspected that the sheriff had spoken to him about what had transpired at the river that day and perhaps advised Major that a visit to Atlanta might well place his errant son in good stead. After all, "idle hands" and the like.

I did not mind being shuttled off to Atlanta that way, to tell you the truth, for the trip gave me an opportunity to do some serious reflecting upon my future. Besides, it would offer me a chance to spend some time with my cousin Robert, my Uncle John, and my Aunt Permelia, with whom I always enjoyed our shared company.

Over the next several days, my Uncle John advised me of the values of continuing my education as something preferable—I imagine—to wandering the streets and back alleyways of downtown Valdosta and taking random potshots at recalcitrant Negroes. I told him that I was interested in learning to become a doctor, as he had done. But he had all but given up medicine for a living by that time, concentrating instead on his partnership in a local business in Atlanta, a grocery and dry-goods shop called Tidwell and Holliday, where he made more money than he ever had as an MD.

He said that doctoring as a profession had lost its allure for him, what with the loosening of medical standards for passing the professional exam to the point where nearly any quack could hang out his shingle; and respectable doctors were forced to compete with charlatans and con men on equal ground. Why, even the relatively upstart specialty practice of dentistry, my uncle said, had surpassed the medical physician's profession in stature within the public's eyes. Dentists were using progressive anesthetic techniques involving ether and nitrous oxide to provide for painless treatment and extractions—something many doctors of the day still frowned upon. Don't ask me why. Perhaps because they could extract more money from conscious patients than from unconscious ones. *No doubt,* my uncle had said decidedly; dentistry was by far the more progressive discipline of the two and the more deserving of my consideration.

Valuing my uncle's advice such as I did, I indeed agreed to avail myself of the many talents and the advanced educational opportunities that the fine art of dentistry would provide me. After further discussion we decided that the best schools for dentistry were in the North, a conclusion I was slow to embrace. But in time I realized that my uncle was right.

The South, and Atlanta in particular, was still reeling from its losses to the war. Reconstructionists and carpetbaggers were plying their wiles everywhere. While the South was rebuilding its institutions one structure at a time, the North had managed to retain its tradition of excellence in education, which supremacy had remained virtually unchanged since before the war. So it was with a great deal of resign that, when I asked my uncle what schools he thought best suited for my studies, he recommended the University of Pennsylvania and, nearby, the Pennsylvania College of Dental Surgery, and my future had been set.

I would return to Valdosta to discuss the matter with my father, whom I knew would be anxious to see me off to further my education, if not for other less noble reasons.

But when I returned home, I found things little changed as when I had left them. In part, I had myself to blame for that. I had been and still remained a by-product of the Reconstruction period—I hated everything about it. I hated the fact that we had lost the war, and that now the North had sent its federal employees into our backyards and, so it seemed, into our very homes to help put us back on the righteous path toward national reunification. It was as though they treated us as children. My father, I felt, had not taken up a strong enough position against Reconstruction and, in fact, stood squarely in support of it as a means toward financial gain: He saw the unification of North and South as an expansion of the marketplace, which could only be of marked benefit to himself and his new family.

So when I learned shortly after returning to Valdosta that some of my friends had developed a plan to blow up the Lowndes County Court House, which housed the Freedmen's Bureau, the despised arm of the Reconstruction movement responsible for overseeing the rights of the freed slaves (an ideal that defiled traditional white southern philosophy), I foolishly decided to join in.

It would be an act of absolute defiance by a cocksure young man absolutely defiant to the North's oft-stated goals of pulling my beloved Southland to its bosom and making it, once again, a poor cousin to the North's wealthy industrialists.

By this, I could not abide.

So I joined in their ranks, these neighbors and friends and co-conspirators, and would have probably gone through with the plot but for the fact that a number of our friends and neighbors caught word of the plan and made it clear to us that they would be in the courthouse on the designated night to hear a political speaker. Any act against the building, they announced, would be an act against them.

The kegs of powder that we had secretly placed beneath the courthouse were just as secretly removed.

Somehow, of course, my father caught wind of the entire incident—I do believe the man had personal spies in my very bedroom—and although he was originally skeptical about sending a son of his to study in the North, he suddenly decided that the notion had more than a modicum of merit to it.

Shortly thereafter, I was on the train headed east and then north to Philadelphia, and my head was filled with both fear and trepidation, as well as more than a little amount of hope for the future.

Now, I understood and understand to this day that some people might consider a professional occupation that requires the insertion of one's hands into the mouth of another to be unsavory, but I thoroughly enjoyed the notion. What greater power can one man have over another but to grab control of him from the inside out?

Thus it was in September 1870, I arrived in Philadelphia, the City of Brotherly Love and absolutely the most astonishing place I had ever visited in my life, veritably bustling with activity, to begin my education as a dentist extraordinaire.

I was off to a good start.

The Pennsylvania College of Dental Surgery was generally regarded as one of the best dental schools in the country, if not the world. Housed in an imposing building at the comer of Twelfth and Filbert streets, it was an outgrowth of the Philadelphia College of Dental Surgery, whose charter extended back to 1850. The Pennsylvania College had been chartered six years later, following a schism between the trustees and the faculty of the older college that had resulted in the faculty resigning en masse in order to create the new institution.

I began my studies there on October 3, 1870. The college had an average number of students of from fifty to sixty. I attended daily lectures and demonstrations both mornings and afternoons and began immediately to participate in clinical procedures under the direction of various dental practitioners. It was a rigorous schedule, six days a week, but one that suited my needs. As a stranger in the city, my free-time requirements were understandably limited. And with the city being a major hub of activity, we were never at a loss for new patients in need of free dental work.

One of those patients whom I remember most vividly was a six-year-old girl who had been brought to the school with diseased molars. After taking exacting impressions of the teeth in question, I created a crown of pure swaged gold, which I attached to the child's molars with red copper cement. Although I did not realize it at the time, I eventually learned—long after having exhausted my time here on earth—that the crown remained intact until the girl died a considerably older woman at the age of 102, her J. H. Holliday bridge still intact.

As I grew close to completing my first term at the college, I found myself with increasingly more time on my hands and so took it upon myself to explore the many recreational faculties provided by the city. At first, wandering around the streets of Philadelphia proved intimidating. This was, after all, the very first time in my life that I had ventured outside the Southland and my home in Georgia. Far from the influence of friends and family, it was not surprising to me to learn that I had little penchant for remaining true to my communal standards.

I had found my first whorehouse.

Now, I had not found my first whore, you understand; for whores exist in every community and serve their fair share of purposes equally, if not magnanimously. I confess upon occasion even to having visited one or two in Georgia. But I had never come face-to-face before with an entire building filled to the rafters with the wenches before, and that discovery for a young man far from home and imbued with raging hormones was a welcomed one.

I did not, of course, randomly abandon all of the principles at the root of my moral training. That would have been anathema for a southern Christian gentleman. But I did partake from time to time in the social proclivities afforded by the city's wide range of saloons, dance halls, gambling dens, and brothels.

One such establishment, which eventually grew to become one of my favorite places of sordid, if not totally ill, repute was a two-story brownstone with a storefront that had no store behind its facade. Instead, gentlemen of the city—northern gentlemen, mostly—would be treated upon walking by the establishment to the sight of a bevy of buxom beauties, most between the ages of sixteen and twenty, who would appear at the open windows overlooking the street, call out to the passersby, and wave—some sharing more than a casual glance at their pulchritude.

It is at this particular establishment that I met one particularly young whore who went by the name of Josie. She had run away from home, an often recounted story (whether true or not, I could never determine), at an early age and made her way to the city, where she was quick to attach herself to a woman who went by the name of Belle, another oft-recounted tale. Josie claimed to be eighteen when I met her, and she quickly proved to be a welcomed relief to the rigors and demands of my studies. Despite her young age, she taught an eager young man what joys and infinite pleasures are to be had in the embrace of femininity, and I shall never forget her for her kindness and patience.

But lest you get the impression that I had suddenly turned from a quiet Christian gentleman into a demon of sex-crazed lust, let me assure you I had not. I spent in total perhaps five or six evenings with Josie, and once with another woman by the name of Bess or Tess or something of the sort, although she was too large-framed a woman to be of more than a passing interest to me. Besides, my position at the college demanded that I be discrete in my dealings outside of the classroom, and for most of my five-month term there, I remained so.

When at last my term had ended, I was enjoined to spend some time with a practicing dentist as an assistant, learning on the job, as it were, from his personal and professional tutorage. Although the college normally arranged for such training for its students, I chose instead to return to Valdosta where I began studying under an admirably efficient dentist by the name of Dr. Lucian Frederick Frink, with whom I remained for eight months.

Frink was a friend of my father. Both had been officers in the Valdosta Chapter of the Royal Arch Masons. It is through that relationship that Dr. Frink came to accept the responsibility of serving as my preceptor.

I remained in Valdosta, staying at Dr. Frink's two-story home—a fine antebellum building with elaborate oak-and-cypress wood trimmings and a bust of Napoleon Bonaparte featured on the stairwell landing leading to the upper floor, until October of that year, when I returned to Philadelphia to resume my studies. As part of the requirements for matriculation, I was to write a thesis related to dentistry. I settled upon the topic of "Diseases of the Teeth," and I completed my paper to the great adulation of my instructors. I was graduated on March 1, 1872, with the degree of Doctor of Dental Surgery.

By that time I had consumed my fill of northern life, and I eagerly departed the city once again for the more familiar surroundings of home. My Uncle John and Aunt Permelia invited me to become a part of the Holliday household at 66 Forrest Avenue in Atlanta, and I eagerly accepted their invitation while establishing myself in my new career.

Although officially a graduated dentist, the state law of Georgia required that candidates for certification be twenty-one years of age. I was still five months shy. As a result, I had to work as a dental assistant until August 1872, when I finally received my credentials.

Alas, while the company amongst whom I lived proved to be predictably charming, the times in Georgia were changing. Reconstruction officially ended on January 12, 1872, after which my uncles, Tom and

William McKey, bought more land at the confluence of the Little and Withlacoochee rivers. While I could have chosen to return to Valdosta to practice with Dr. Frink and enjoy the company of my relatives, I realized by then that my future no longer lay in Georgia.

With some time on my hands and a world of discovery awaiting me, I decided to travel to St. Louis, Missouri, where one of my classmates had recently opened his practice. A. Jameson Fuches Jr., who wrote his thesis on the same topic as did I, had opened an office on Fourth Street, and I soon enough joined him there. St. Louis was a bustling, hardy, bawdy place, the gateway to the West, filled with all sorts of delights for a young, unmarried professional man such as myself. Working under Fuches allowed me the opportunity to gain experience in my chosen profession, as well as in other matters less professionally inclined.

Around the corner from Fuches's office stood a theater and a saloon. One of the employees there was a young woman named Kate Fisher, but that was not her real name. She was born Mary Katharine (or Katherine) Harony in Pest, Hungary, on November 7, 1850, the first of seven children. Her parents had immigrated to the United States around 1860, just as the Civil War broke out, and settled in Davenport, Iowa, with what amounted to a colony of other Hungarian immigrants. Kate's father had purchased property there in 1863, but by 1866 both he and his wife had died, leaving the care of the minor Harony children under the guardianship of their brother-in-law, Gustavus Susemihl. Guardianship soon passed to the family attorney, Otto Smith, who reported in October 1867 that Mary Katharine could not be advised of the mortgage of the family's property "because she went, as it is said, to parts unknown."

In fact, Kate had run away. She took the last name of Fisher after one of the leading actresses of the day, Kate Fisher, whose performances as Mazeppa, in which she rode across the stage on horseback wearing only pink tights, scandalized and tantalized audiences across the nation. Kate claimed to have entered a convent in St. Louis, but like many runaway girls of that day, she actually entered a considerably "different" school.

A woman by the name of "Kate Fischer" was subsequently listed in the 1870 official St. Louis census living with eight other women. Seven of them, including Kate, were listed as "whores." By 1872 she was working at the saloon near Dr. Fuches's new office.

Kate told the story years afterward that, while in St. Louis, she had married a dentist by the name of Silas Melvin and that the two had a son. Subsequently, she said that both husband and son died of yellow fever.

But that was not exactly true. No record exists that supports the marriage, the birth of a child, or the deaths of either Melvin *or* a child. What I do know through my countless inquiries over the years is that a man who went by the name of Silas Melvin did indeed live in St. Louis in the mid-1860s, but he was married to a steamship captain's daughter by the name of Mary Bust. The city census further showed that Melvin's occupation was not a dentist but an employee at a St. Louis asylum.

Of course, Kate's recollection of events long since past have proven over the years to be not without flaw. Likewise her penchant for telling the truth. She often mixed one event with another so as to produce deliberately a hybrid of them both that more precisely fit her needs at the moment. Her quick wits and fascination with fantasy are two of the things that would eventually endear me to her. *Eventually.*

I did find a woman in St. Louis who proved to be as charming a whore and well educated a young woman as I had ever met, albeit somewhat rough around the edges, with steely eyes and a will to match. She always had a smile for me when I walked into her establishment, which I believe at the time was run by the one and only Bessie Earp, the wife of Wyatt's brother James. The two of us spent an afternoon playing cards and drinking together and quickly became good friends. Not long afterwards, we became more than that, as she laid herself bare for me late one evening after she had finished her work. I accounted well of myself, thanks in part to my previous liaisons in Philadelphia— so well so that she told me that she thought she might be falling in love with me.

All of that was nonsense, I realized. We had barely grown to know one another; and if I were to fall in love with a woman in so short a period of time, I vowed that she would not be a whore. So when it came time to part—my uncle having written me to return to Georgia to claim my share of inheritance left to me upon my mother's passing—I was able to do so with no sign of the tears that showed in her own eyes. She told me that she would never forget Doctor John H. Holliday, nor— little though this cocksure, overinflated, egotistic young man realized at the time—would I, her.

Following my return home, I was introduced to Dr. Arthur C. Ford, one of the most prominent dentists in the state. Ford was an Englishman who had come to Georgia by way of South Africa. He had fought gallantly in the Confederate army, was wounded at Sharpsburg, and had established himself as a dentist in Atlanta after the war as the partner of Dr. Albert Hape. After Hape had terminated his partnership with Ford and decided to move his practice to Thomson, Georgia, Dr. Ford ran this notice in the *Atlanta Constitution:*

> I HEREBY inform my patients that I leave to attend the Sessions of the Southern Dental Association in Richmond, Virginia this evening, and will be absent until about the middle of August, during which time Dr. Jno. H. Holliday will fill my place in my office.
>
> *Arthur C. Ford, D.D.S.*
> *Office 26, Whitehall Street.*83

It was a grand opportunity for me. Dr. Ford's prominence ensured the right connections and the best chances for my success in my own hometown. I remember turning twenty-one upon the very day that Dr. Ford returned to Atlanta, and less than a month later, my father signed over the property he had held in guardianship for me since my mother's death.

My future seemed bright.

In November I traveled to Griffin to register my deed for the Iron Front Building. I had at last come of age, and for the occasion, my uncle presented me with a Model 1851 Navy Colt revolver like those he had given to his own three sons. I had good reason to be proud. Never quite feeling the role of the Southern aristocrat, I was now fairly enjoined a gentleman of the South, well bred, educated, and prepared for the successful professional life I had trained for as an integral part of the Reconstruction.

But be that as it may, I could not get the thought of my St. Louis dalliance out of my mind, the woman whose memory lingered in my thoughts almost from the day upon which I had left the city for good. I could not get over her, and I could not get over something else that I had noticed occurring with increasing frequency. Something that would become a fortuitous turn of fortune for some. And anything but for others.

Affirmations

DEPOSITION

Wyatt Earp, Los Angeles, 1926

In 1926, Wyatt Earp, in a deposition in Los Angeles, explained some of the tensions in Tombstone in 1881:

Q After you became Deputy United States Marshal, there was not the best of feeling between your office and the office of the sheriff?

A No.

Q The sheriff's name was Behan?

A Yes.

Q You were allied with one faction and he with another?

A Yes.

Q With you was allied Doc Holliday?

A Yes.

Q He was somewhat of a notorious character in those days?

A Well, no. I couldn't say that he was notorious outside of this other faction trying to make him notorious. Of course he killed a man or two before he went there.

Q Didn't he have the reputation of being a holder-up of stages?

A I never heard of it until I left.

Q With the Behans were allied the Clandens [*sic*]?

A Yes. And the Behan side whenever they got a chance to hurt me over Holliday's shoulders they would do it. They would make a lot of talk about Doc Holliday.

Q Because he was allied with you?

A He never had no trouble in Tombstone outside of being in this street fight [at the O.K. Corral] with us. Then on one occasion he got in trouble with part of the combination that was against me, Joyce, [Behan's] partner, and he shot Joyce in the hand and the other fellow in the foot and of course that made them pretty sore against Holliday. But they knew that I was Holliday's friend and they tried to injure me every way they could. . . . This fellow Behan, he intended to run for sheriff and he knew that I did, and if I do say it myself I was a pretty strong man for the position. He knew that he had to do me some way and he done everything in the world that he could against me. He stood in with this tough element, the Cowboys and stage robbers and others, because they were pretty strong and he wanted their vote. Whenever they would get a chance to shoot anything at me over Holliday's shoulders they would do it. So they made Holliday a bad man. An awful bad man, which was wrong. He was a man that would fight if he had to.

I learned of Wyatt's testimony shortly after he gave it, and he pretty much nailed the coffin tight. Except that I thought he didn't go far enough in laying blame where it squarely belonged.

Yes, it was Johnny Behan allied with the Cowboys who created most of the chaos in Tombstone in those days because, as Wyatt said, he planned on running for sheriff and needed their votes, which were in number considerable. Joyce, whom I shot in that ruckus over at the Oriental Saloon, was with Behan and the Cowboys because he hated the Earps. Wyatt had bought into the Oriental and, as part owner, tried to run a clean house. But Joyce bought out another partner, giving him controlling interest, and forced Wyatt into selling his share in the place. That's when we stopped going there and started hanging out at the pool hall, over at Campbell & Hatch's. After that a bad element pretty much took over at the Oriental, and I tried to stay clear of the place as much as I could, although if there was a big game going on there, I would usually show up.

Where I believe Wyatt failed to come down hard enough was in taking on Behan, who was a cowardly, conniving, backstabbing son of a bitch who never deserved to be sheriff or anything else, so far as I was concerned.

When I at first arrived in Tombstone, I found all of the Earp brothers, including Wyatt, James, Morgan, and Virgil, there. The outlaw Cowboys who saw the Earps as an impediment to their cattle-rustling business out of Mexico included Old Man Clanton and his sons, Ike, Phin, and Billy, plus the McLaury brothers, Frank and Tom, along with Curly Bill Brocius, John Ringo, and several other saddle tramps. These people had for years been riding down into Mexico, rustling cattle, and driving them back into the North to sell for beef, sometimes for as little as $1 a head. It was clear profit.

If anyone had the nerve to question them or the source of their beef, they would threaten to shoot him dead and then follow through on their threats.

This rustling scheme had been going on for years, and everyone knew it, but no one had the courage to stand up to it. That included

John Behan. He threw in with the rustlers, knowing that they were lawbreakers and murderers. When the Earps came to town, they recognized the problems facing the area and swore to put an end to the Cowboys' activities. That's when Behan first openly challenged the Earps' authority and set out to work against them.

When the Kinnear (Benson) stage holdup occurred, during which the driver and another man were killed, I was accused by the Cowboys of planning it. That was humorous to me, as I knew who had really orchestrated the holdup—and it had been those very same cowardly dogs, led by Curly Bill, Ike Clanton, Frank Stilwell, and Pete Spencer, followed by a few more. Why, even Wyatt—Marshal Earp—vouched for me, stating on record that I was in town at the Alhambra Saloon at the time the robbery was reported. I had been in town since late that afternoon, he said, and had been dealing faro at 10 p.m. when the robbery had occurred. And that should have been the end to that.

But a friend of mine, a onetime respected jeweler by the name of Leonard, was named as one of the bandits. That, of course, made the jump between Leonard and me, and the Cowboys presented their "findings" to Sheriff Behan, who was all too happy to spread the rumor that I had been involved. He was a low-life mangy cur. I tell you I had no use for the man at all. And I would most gladly have called him out, as my friend Wyatt should have done.

Have you ever known a scorpion to back down from a challenge?

Have you ever *seen* a scorpion?

The Deadliest Dentist

I know not whence it came, but I do know that my relationship with Dr. Ford did not last long. He was not a well man. As it turned out, he was suffering from consumption, the same disease that had taken my loving mother's life so violently years before; and he announced on January 4, 1873, that he was turning his practice over to Dr. J. Cooley while he went to Florida to take the cure. I had heard that he had subsequently returned to Georgia, where he was elected president of the Georgia State Dental Society later that year and eventually moved permanently to Florida, where I later learned that he died in 1883.

Back at the present, I was disappointed that the good doctor did not offer his practice to me, thinking perhaps that I was too young and too inexperienced to accept so many responsibilities so soon into my career. As Dr. Cooley was not in need of an apprentice at the time, we severed our relationship as amicably as possible.

I decided, as well, that the time had come for me to leave my aunt and uncle's home so as not to become burdensome to them. I registered at the National Hotel in Atlanta shortly before Christmas. It was the darkest holiday season I had ever known.

I received word that my uncle Robert, my cousin Mattie's father, had died. The *Griffin News* carried the announcement, saying, "Mr.

Robert Holliday, who has so long and efficiently occupied the position of baggage master on the Macon & Western Railroad, died at Jonesboro on Christmas night."

Mattie recalled later, "Everything gone but one house in Jonesboro, a large helpless family, health wrecked, it is no wonder this jovial, kindhearted man was heartbroken. Seven years struggle with poverty, he died December 24, 1872, after being received into the Catholic Church. He was buried in the Catholic plot in Fayetteville."

I went to the funeral, of course, in order to help console Mattie, her sisters, and her brother Jim Bob. It was a startlingly somber affair. But it was only the beginning of a bad time in my life. Less than a month later, on January 13, 1873, my step-brother, Francisco Hidalgo, died of consumption on his farm near Jenkinsburg, leaving behind a grieving young family of his own. Although I had not recently been close to him, I loved and respected him for having served honorably in the Confederate Army and for having won the heart and the home of my father, something I felt less accomplished in doing.

The following day, consumed by the tenuousness of life, I sold my half of the Iron Front Building in Griffin, receiving a total of $1,800 for it, and began to give some serious thought to my own tenuous future. I checked into a local hotel and, with my life's savings in tow, set out to drown my sorrows in one of the many bars and gambling houses of the town.

It was in Griffin, under the patient tutelage of several prominent dealers, that I learned to play and, eventually, to deal the game of faro. It was there, too, that I learned that my cousin Robert had decided to follow in my footsteps and attend the Pennsylvania College of Dental Surgery in the fall of 1873. He wrote to ask if I would be his preceptor, and of course I was delighted to accept. We discussed the possibility of our forming a dental partnership once Hub, which was his nickname, was graduated.

But before long—long before the anticipated partnership could be consummated—I went to see my Uncle John about a persistent cough I had developed, one that refused to relinquish itself to the usual remedies of the day. It was from him that I received the news I had already anticipated. Using a stethoscope and a bronchoscope, he diagnosed that I had pulmonary tuberculosis. After watching my mother die, after burying Francisco, and realizing that Dr. Ford was deep within the sinewy grasp of the deadly disease, I came with some degree of finality to accept the fact that I, too, could very well die of consumption.

Now, the term "consumption" means little to the person who does not suffer from the disease. It meant much to me. An insidious and indiscriminate killer, its very name was coined after the manner in which it works its deed: consuming the body from within, slowly, one day at a time, until there is nothing left of a person's lungs and emaciated body to remain to fight yet one more minute. I watched it firsthand claim my mother's life, ever so slowly, and hated it vehemently for what it had done to her.

Yet, I saw firsthand how my mother fought against it. How she refused to believe that it would win out in the end. To the consumptive patient, nothing is so plainly etched in the mind as the possibility for a cure. A miracle. A remission. So slowly does the disease progress that, day after day, one begins to believe that there is hope. *I am no worse today than I was yesterday and, in fact, perhaps a little better.* That is the maddening thing about having the disease. How you can range from the very depths of hell to the thought that you have fought it off and won.

So, after talking with my uncle, he suggested a prescription consisting of warm, dry air combined with a good diet, a modicum of red wine, and prolonged rest as a period of convalescence. There was a growing view among physicians that such a regimen offered the best opportunity to turn tuberculosis into remission and that the disease need not be a death knell. My family both hoped and prayed for a complete recovery. I was squarely behind them.

My uncle called the entire family together, and we decided that my cousin Robert would continue with his plans to attend dental school, selecting a replacement for the preceptor that he would require before graduation. I was to go west, the sooner the better. But where west?

Charles Nordholl, a traveler and onetime managing editor of the *New York Evening Post,* had recently published a volume called *California: For Health, Pleasure and Residence.* The author told how southern California, in particular, was a welcome relief for consumptives, relaying the tale of a neighbor who had struggled for life at Aiken, South Carolina. Barely after arriving in California, he "ate heartily and slept well, enjoyed his life, and coughed hardly at all."

That was all my uncle had to hear. It was off to California for young Doc Holliday.

My father, though, who had seen more of the world than my uncle, argued that many regions west of the Mississippi River offered comparable climates to that of southern California. One of them was Dallas, Texas, which had the advantage of being much closer to home and more accessible to friends and family.

The decision was made finally. While Robert completed dental school, I would travel to Dallas, where I would convalesce. By the time Robert's education was completed, I would be healed and ready, at last, to join him in our mutual careers.

I discussed with doctors Ford and Samuel Hape my plans, and the latter recommended to me a Dr. John A. Seegar, a prominent dentist, as someone with whom I could work while convalescing. I wrote Dr. Seegar, enclosing a letter of introduction from Hape and of recommendation from Ford. Dr. Seegar must have been impressed, since he wrote back quickly, offering me a position as partner in his dental practice once I arrived in Dallas.

So it came to be that, on a hot and humid morning in September 1873, as the family gathered at the Western and Atlantic Depot to see me off, I shook hands with my cousin Robert and hugged Aunt Permelia and Uncle John, who gave me a small package that was wrapped in tissue paper. I quickly tore the paper off and opened the box.

"Oh, my," I said. "It's beautiful."

Uncle John smiled at me. "It's a diamond stickpin," he said. "Wear it always. If you ever get in trouble, remember that you can always cash it in."

I could never have anticipated such an extravagant gift and had to fight back the tears as I closed the box and tucked it into my vest pocket.

I shook hands with my father and hugged Sophie, our slave, who fought hard the losing battle in holding her own tears back. Afterward, I mounted the steps to the coach and, as the early morning clock swung 'round toward 8:30, settled into my seat to begin my trip west.

It was the beginning of a new chapter in the life of Dr. John Henry Holliday, DDS. It was more than a new chapter; it was the dawn of a new life for a young consumptive otherwise destined for death.

I was filled with excitement as the train left the last remnants of the city behind and cut its path across the prairies and woods outside of town. I was filled with hope and enthusiasm, as well, and adventure. Here I was, barely twenty-one years of age, and setting out on the journey of a lifetime.

I hoped that it would be a long, prosperous, and healthy one.

Westward Bound

HAPPY NEW YEAR!

Dallas Weekly Herald, *January 2, 1875*

D r. Holliday and Mr. [Charles W.] Austin, a saloon keeper, relieved the monotony of the noise of firecrackers by taking a couple of shots at each other yesterday afternoon. The cheerful note of the peaceful six shooter is heard once more among us. Both shooters were arrested.

As a rule, I did not mind traveling by rail, as it certainly was kinder on one's kidneys than traveling by stage. But by the end of my second day away from home, the countless miles of open prairie land and wilderness that winked at me through the window began to meld into a solid panorama of despair. Once you have seen Tennessee grasslands for more than three hundred miles, you have seen all grasslands everywhere, enough for a lifetime.

I did not object to visiting in Chattanooga, Memphis, or New Orleans, where I managed to steal some time to myself, long enough at least to visit a local establishment for the eradication of the terminally parched. An hour later and I was back onboard, rambling over the countryside once again, this time headed for Morgan City, from where I was forced to take a stagecoach to Beaumont, Texas. From Beaumont, the Texas and New Orleans Railroad took me to the rattling cow town of Houston, from which I boarded the H and TC for the final leg of my journey.

I finally pulled the last leg of my trip from Georgia into Dallas to begin my work as a dentist resplendent in the practice of Dr. John A. Seegar in the third week of September 1873. I was not sorry to see my journey come to an end. In fact, everything considered, I was grateful to be alive. It had been well over a week since I had bid my family goodbye. It had been over a week since I had left everyone and everything I loved in a cloud of steam and a belch of cinders headed toward God only knew what.

Upon my disembarkation in Dallas, I recognized immediately what everyone had been writing about in the newspapers back east. The lazy town of not more than a few hundred people had soared to a major metropolis of more than seven thousand in less than a year since the railroad had laid a spur through the town. In order to service all of those people, more than seven hundred buildings had been constructed, with new businesses popping up daily. Dry-goods stores, millineries, saloons, gambling houses, hotels, restaurants. If someone anywhere within a hundred miles needed anything, you could damned well be sure that someone in Dallas had just opened his doors to accommodate him.

That, quite naturally, included dentists, which made my move to the Texas city all that much more alluring. Dr. Seegar, who had hung out his shingle in March 1869, quite literally could not keep up with the influx of new business he experienced daily and so was relieved to have found a new partner—and someone who came, as I do not mind telling you, so highly recommended as myself. There existed only four dental offices in the entire city, including Seegar's practice. I had arrived just in time to be included in the 1873 edition of Lawson and Edmondson's *Dallas City Directory*. It was a daisy. I was officially a Texan.

I made certain, of course, that Dr. Seegar was not disappointed in his choice of an associate. My erudite sophistication, Southern manners, genteel nature, and refined good looks appealed to him instantly. He let me know in no uncertain terms that I would have no trouble in finding and keeping a loyal constituency of patients.

Dr. Seegar had been the first person I spoke to at the depot when I arrived, and I took a liking to him immediately. He was tall, somewhat heavier than I, several years older, and clean shaven. Everything considered, he reminded me of a barber I had known back in Griffin. I had taken an immediate liking to *him*, too.

Without much ado, the good doctor took me straight away to become acquainted with the rest of my new family at the Seegar home on Boll Street just south of Ross Avenue. He poured us both a glass of Port in anticipation of dinner, and John—for that is what he insisted that I call him—advised me on how he had brought his teenage bride, Martha, to Dallas from Georgia before the war. She had since gone on to birth him five children, the oldest of whom had barely reached twelve years of age. My arrival in Texas brought John not only some welcomed relief from the hectic schedule at which he toiled six days out of the week, but also news of the progress wrought by Reconstruction in our home state of Georgia.

The following day, I wasted little time in receiving introductions at Dr. Seegar's office. It was located at 56 Elm St., which along with Main Street, made up the city's two main thoroughfares. Dr. Seegar's office— excuse me, I mean, *our* office—was situated above Dr. A. M. Cochran's drugstore between Market and Austin streets, exactly one mile from the Seegar home. John had already had the sign out front repainted to read Seegar and Holliday. It was a beautiful sight.

And so, with but a handshake between us, we embarked upon our professional partnership. Dr. Seegar shortly thereafter informed me that he intended to introduce me to Dallas at the annual fair of the North Texas agricultural mechanical and blood Stock Association. It seemed a strange place for introductions, in the midst of the Dallas County Fairgrounds, but John had devised a plan wherein we would enter the exhibition to show off our finest work. As I unpacked some of the exhibits that I had previously prepared for my professors at dental school, Dr. Seegar was impressed. He suggested that we use them as our entries, and I was flattered he thought so highly of them.

So, on Tuesday, September 30, we entered our exhibits. On Friday, October 3, we returned to the Dallas fairgrounds in time to hear the announcer call out the awards. Doctors Seegar and Holliday swept the competition. We won three premium prizes of a plate and $5 for each of our displays. These included the best set of teeth in gold, the best in vulcanized rubber, and the best set of artificial teeth and dental ware.

John, of course, was thrilled to see our new partnership get off to such a fine start. Obviously, I was elated, especially after having been forced to leave a very promising dental career in Atlanta. Perhaps, I thought, the prizes were symbolic of greater things to come. Perhaps my decision to travel west was already beginning to pay off.

As I continued to settle into my new household, the Seegars invited me to join them on their Sunday outings to the Baptist church to which they belonged. I respectfully declined their invitations, however, since as one of my mother's last wishes I had joined the congregation of the Rev. R. W. Thompson's Methodist Episcopal church. I went so far as to become a prominent member of a temperance organization. At least I did until I came to my senses and leaped off that wagon of rectitude.

I had barely gotten used to my new surroundings on Boll Street when, on Wednesday, October 8, I heard people running through town, shouting that fire had broken out near our office. The Kentucky Store, which was situated at the corner of Main and Market Streets barely a block from Cochran's drugstore, had burst aflame, and the sparks were threatening the entire block. A strong southeast wind placed most of the wood-framed buildings in town in danger. The local fire department sent out a hook and ladder company that arrived promptly on the scene but was unable to contain the inferno. By that afternoon, one entire block bounded by Maine, Market, Elm, and Jefferson streets had been destroyed. Leveled. Smoldering. Nothing was left, save for a few brick chimneys. Fortunately for us, Cochran's drugstore lay just east of the fire's limits and out of its reach. *Unfortunately,* at least in the judgment of the city's sporting crowd, the Alhambra Saloon located on Elm Street did not fare so well.

The city set about recovering from the fire and continued its expansion of the past year and a half into the fall. That's when the panic of 1873, which had started with the overconstruction of the railroads, brought about one of the country's greatest recessions. The slumping economy put a halt to the immigration of the nation's populace to many of the railroad cities, including Dallas. The Texas and Pacific hubbed there was no exception. The recession would remain in Texas for the next seven years, with an influx of only three thousand additional people moving to Dallas throughout that entire time.

Of course, my continuing battle with consumption, along with the city's deepening financial woes, made it increasingly difficult for me to earn a living from my practiced profession. I found myself with a great deal of leisure time on my hands, which I used to expand my social circle beyond that of the Seegar family. It did not take me long to discover the St. Charles saloon on Main Street, where the gaming tables were particularly popular with the locals. I was also known to frequent the Alhambra Saloon, which had rebuilt following the fire in an excellent location on the corner of Main and Houston streets, opposite the Crutchfield House, one of Dallas's finest hotels. That and Johnny Thompson's Bella Union served as headquarters for the majority of the local gaming populace.

Naturally, the town's faro bankers welcomed me with open arms. They should have known better, being generally ill-advised of my training in the sport of card playing at the hands of Sophie, our slave, back at our home in Georgia. I very quickly observed the similarities between the old slave game of "Skinning" and the age-old game of faro. Faro was quite a bit easier to learn, because the case keeper kept track of the cards in the discard pile, providing no advantage to the dealer. Or at least not so in an honest game. But I soon discovered that honest games were few and far between in Dallas. In time I would learn that much for myself. The hard way.

In many respects, I had a lot to learn about gambling Texas-style. And I was nothing if not an adept pupil. I learned, for example, that the country's largest and best-known manufacturer of gaming equipment published a national catalog featuring prominent displays of faro layouts. The vast majority of dealing boxes listed in their catalog were rigged for "dealing seconds," one method of crooked dealing designed to separate the player from his cash.

Another item in their catalog was a fine line of card-trimming shears, used to prolong the life of playing cards by trimming off the frayed edges. Of course, all but the most fledgling of gamblers knew that they were used for another purpose as well—trimming the edges of certain denominations of cards in order to differentiate them from the others, which knowledge gave the faro banker an advantage in a game in which he otherwise had none.

There were large numbers of other devices used by both dealers and players, including numerous varieties of marked cards, holdouts, nail picks, and even vest cold-decking machines that allowed the wearer to exchange an entire deck of cards without being caught.

The fierce competition of the games in the kitchen of Uncle John's home in Atlanta, where Sophie, Robert, George, and I had come to recognize a few of the sleight-of-hand tricks used by many faro bankers, had prepared me well to test my mettle at the tables out West. It was called *mechanics,* the way in which dealers gave the advantage in a game to themselves. In the West, cheating was commonplace, and often accepted, especially among inexperienced players. While I was no stranger to this preconception, my innate good sense forced me to shy away from any dishonest efforts, at least until I had grown skilled enough not to get caught.

I was also fortunate enough to have been blessed with a mathematical mind, which made it easy for me to compute the odds of certain cards being turned up. Based upon the discards, I found it a relatively simple matter to anticipate what the dealer would do next. To me, it was simply a matter of technique.

Once I had made myself known to my new community, not only as the new dentist in town but also as one of its most enthusiastic gaming men, it seems that I was never lacking for good company. Before long

I was providing myself with a respectable supplemental income from my sport as both a faro player and banker, and as a poker player of some success. I eventually purchased my own faro layout that included a case-keeper dealing box, as well as a fine pair of Will and Finck card-trimming shears.

I had a marked advantage over most other gamblers at the table whenever I played. I was good at what I did, of course; but I also had my income from my dentistry to use as a bankroll. At first, my professional income was by far the greater of the two, but in time, as my practice dwindled, so too did my dentistry income, which I was able through skill and wit to replace with my gaming-table earnings. In fact, by March of 1874, my gambling income far exceeded the paltry few dollars I still managed to make from dentistry.

It is not that I was not a good dentist, you understand, for I was. But between the downturn in the economic fortunes of the townsfolk and the difficulty I had in catering to patients in between my coughing fits, dentists no longer seemed to be first and foremost on people's minds. At least, not *this* dentist.

Not that it bothered me all that much. I enjoyed my newly evolving lifestyle ever so much more than practicing dentistry. Where else can a man pit himself against the cards and one another, against Lady Luck and his own skill and intellect and emerge victorious? And while you're at it, has the saloon owner or the faro banker continued to buy you all the liquor you could possibly hold, while some pretty young thing brought the bottle around and smiled lasciviously at you every quarter hour on the hour?

So it was not totally unexpected when Dr. Seegar approached me one morning and suggested to me that we might be better off, the two of us, if we mutually agreed to dissolve our partnership and go our separate ways. I do believe that, in addition to the pecuniary rationale behind such an action, he had also grown somewhat apprehensive about the image of any partner of his keeping such ungodly hours in so many of the dens of inequity I confess to have haunted. You don't stumble across many senators and congressmen in seamy back-alley whorehouses, and you don't find many bloated and cash-rich ramrods spending their money at the opera house. *Is est via of orbis terrarum:* It is the way of the world.

So, on March 2, 1874, Dr. Seegar and yours truly parted ways. I moved my practice down the street a few doors, to the second story of the Dallas County Bank at the corner of Main and Lamar streets, where I also took up temporary residence. I am certain that the good doctor had no second thoughts about our decision when, that following May, the town fathers succumbed to pressure from the editor of the *Dallas Weekly Herald* and authorized the local constables to run a sweep of all the local "sporting" houses. Naturally, I was arrested.

It was a little play that I came to understand (some months later) that the marshal ran periodically. When the pressure for action against the illegal sporting establishments grew too strong to ignore, he would round up the gamblers and hurry them into court, where they would smile knowingly, plead guilty, pay a $10 fine, and leave.

I, on the other hand, chose to post a $100 surety bond guaranteeing my future day in court and was allowed to go about my business, which I did for most of the next month until another fire broke out. This one was far more devastating than the first. It occurred in the rear of the new brick building owned and occupied by Johnny Thompson of the Bella Union Saloon. An unsuccessful attempt at arson had been thwarted two nights earlier when restaurant employees doused the flames of a fire. This time, the arsonist had greater success.

The first indication of the fire was a loud explosion followed by the clanging of the firehouse bell. As we rushed out into the street to see what had transpired, I was amazed to find much of the block bounded by Main, Austin, Elm, and Market Streets ablaze. Unfortunately for John Seegar, the area this time included Cochraine's Drug Store and John's second-floor office.

When the next day John and I stood in the street, surveying the carnage, I asked him what he planned to do. He said that he had already decided to open temporary facilities on the corner of Pacific and Market streets.

"John," I said, laying my hand upon the table. "You are going to need new equipment if you are to reopen your practice. I would be willing to sell you mine."

He seemed surprised. "Which equipment would you sell?"

I looked at him squarely. "All of it."

––––––––––

I had notified my family of my change of address to Denison, Texas. Denison was a small town and it was beginning to thrive as the terminus for the Missouri, Kansas and Texas Railroad. I'm not sure what the big attraction was, for I found it to be relatively repulsive as a place to hang one's hat. In fact, it was generally regarded as the lowest of the low Texas towns in regard to its bawdy houses, dance halls, and the variety shows put on there. I personally did not find the town to have many redeeming qualities whatsoever, except perhaps that it was relatively near to my previous home of Dallas, so I often traveled by rail back to the big city in order to meet with old friends, engage in a friendly game or two of faro, and escape my more permanent, if mundane, lifestyle.

In 1875, at the ripe old age of twenty-three, little more than a year out of dental school and recently departed from my beloved home state of Georgia, I was barely intelligent enough to be dangerous. I was also suffering from pulmonary tuberculosis, a disease commonly called in the day consumption, of which at the time there was little concrete medical knowledge and for which there was even less hope of cure.

Worse, still, this disease had taken my mother's life. I had little doubt that, left unattended, it would treat me in kind.

My family, being well grounded within the medical profession, decided that a trip out west, with its drier climate, might place an abatement upon my symptoms and perhaps even precipitate a cure. That is how I ended up traveling to Texas, hanging out my shingle, and opening my dental practice.

I knew instinctively that I would be a good dentist. I was good at most everything I set myself out upon. But my disease, which sometimes caused me to cough a great deal in sudden and violent spasms, was hardly conducive to my budding young practice. Can you imagine someone standing over you with his hands in your mouth, overtaken suddenly by an uncontrollable coughing jag? Certainly my patients must have found such tumultuous fits unnerving. For that reason alone, my practice was not growing as fast as I had hoped, and I was not earning enough from dentistry to see me through life. When I early on found myself in need of extra funds, I set about satisfying it.

Like many people who have traveled before me, I quickly learned that I had a talent at the gaming tables frequented so often by people having far too much money and taking far too little care toward retaining it. My game of choice was faro, in which I excelled dealing, with Spanish monte a close second; although, if they were unavailable to me, I was not averse to playing a hand or two of poker. I had been blessed with a naturally mathematical mind, so I could quickly calculate percentages and count cards, giving me a great advantage over the vast majority of the louts who stumbled through the front doors in order to make their bankrolls available to me.

My gaming skills set me apart from my colleagues in yet another way: I did not have to cheat to win, as most professional gamers of the day did. I could play and win entirely by the luck of the draw combined with my keen ability to analyze and handicap nearly any hand.

Of course, I will not say that I was entirely averse to taking an unfair advantage when dealing faro, as no self-respecting faro dealer is. Faro is a game in which slight of hand can benefit the house tremendously, but I seldom felt the need to resort to such chicanery, and my play was almost always aboveboard.

Shortly after broadening my skills from dentist to gambler, I realized the advantages to moving around the country more frequently than the average DDS. It took little time for my skills to be brought to the attention of the local players—and oftentimes to the constabulary, who often found it difficult to believe that I had come upon my successes honestly.

Of course, honest or not, when you have a good run in gambling, sooner or later you are going to have to defend yourself from the inevitable accusations of fraud. What a humorous call I often found that to be—cheaters calling the one honest man at the table a cheat.

Nevertheless, at nearly six feet in height and ghostly thin, riddled by a peripatetic tubercular cough, when push came to shove, I knew that physical prowess would not be enough to save the day. At such times I felt the desirability to rely upon the tools of my trade—*all* of the tools—which is why I carried for my personal protection a knife and at least one pistol in a shoulder holster, and sometimes an additional six-shooter on my hip. Not surprisingly, when I was brought up in a town on gambling charges, they were usually accompanied by charges of assault and battery or carrying a deadly weapon. And occasionally worse. I did not enjoy being the provocateur, I assure you. But as a matter purely of survival, I rose to the occasion of self-defense whenever necessary.

My good friend, Wyatt Earp, who was no stranger to the use of firearms himself, once wrote of me, "Doc Holliday is the nerviest, speediest, and deadliest man with a gun I have ever seen," although, if truth be known, I drew my weapon relatively rarely, considering that I enjoyed such a formidable reputation, and not always with the most impressive of results.

Part of the reason for this was another attribute of consumption: When I gambled, I drank. Doing so helped relieve me of the boredom of life and satiate the pain and hardships of coping with my disease. That is another thing that I learned about traveling to the West from the South: Whiskey helped to calm my cough, allowing me to remain under control of my own wretched body more so than when I was abstinent.

But alas, it is common sense: The more I drank, the less effective I became with my weapons. Perhaps that was a blessing in disguise, though, for I rarely drank alone, and I always saw to it that I drank less than anyone I might eventually end up throwing my pistol to in the shank of the evening. You would be amazed at just how poorly some of the largest and surliest of bullies could handle their liquor.

Not that I was always drunk whenever I drew my pistol. Wyatt and I would occasionally ride out into the country in the mornings to practice shooting. He saw me draw and fire with no other witnesses around, as I saw him. He was a formidable pistoleer. But I was faster and more accurate than he. And he knew it. We both kept that fact to ourselves, though. I saw no reason to do otherwise, although I saw no earthly reason to prevent others from spreading rumors of my quickness on the draw or my accuracy of shot. By one account, I had savagely shot and killed more than twenty men. That rumor alone had kept at least a few toughs from drawing upon me and saved my worthless hide on several occasions.

Contrary to my growing reputation as a *shootist*, I made a point of drawing only in self-defense, to which effect most court records and other documents will attest. Even the scurrilous lawman Bat Masterson, for whom I had little of merit to say when I was alive and will not change my predilections now, admitted that whenever I got into gun trouble, I was in the right more often than not.

So on that day of the celebration of the arrival of the new year, 1875, when I found myself as usual embroiled in a heated game of chance in the Oriental Saloon and gaming establishment, and Champagne Charlie Austin belittled my gambling acuity in front of a dozen other players, I found myself in a quandary.

Austin was a large, round, and affable gentleman who, when he was sober, was a good enough sort. He was an excellent mixologist, serving up whatever it is you wanted to drink in quick time. He had a reputation, however, for being a "rollicking fellow," which sometimes got him into trouble. The previous year, he had been arrested for intent to commit murder after an attack on the ex-marshal of Dallas, Major G. W. Campbell, although a jury eventually acquitted him. Why, I do not know.

On this particular evening, however, when he attempted to disparage not only myself but my familial lineage, no jury was present to save him. I had taken enough.

"You are a drunken lout, and if I were you, I would keep my jack-asinine feelings to myself. I assure you that, in so doing, you will live longer."

For some reason, Austin took umbrage at my remark and drew upon me, at which time I threw back my chair, jumped to my feet, and began firing away in the general direction of his ugly face.

Fortunately for me, in returning fire, he was in as poor control of his faculties as was I—and even less so—and the two of us merely succeeded in fanning the air for several seconds.

Naturally, that did not prevent the both of us from being arrested, although Champagne Charlie—far better known and more popular in town than I—was not held. I, on the other hand, fared less favorably. A couple of weeks later, a bill of indictment charged me with the crime of assault and attempted murder. Can you imagine? It had been issued by the Dallas County grand jury in connection with the shooting. One week after that, on January 25, I appeared in court to defend myself against the charge. After hearing the evidence against me, the jury retired and soon returned with a verdict of not guilty. Some people think it's strange that the only incident of a shooting in which I was ever involved in the entire state of Texas never occurred until after I had moved out of Dallas.

Even though found not guilty, I had a difficult time enjoying my work in Dallas after that. It is as if the town had suddenly closed in on me, as if the world was getting wise. Not only that, but the thick damp air of Texas had failed to provide the promised relief from my symptoms, which seemed to be growing worse by the week.

All in all, I reasoned, it seemed like a good time to move on.

I returned to Denison shortly thereafter but soon came to realize that the town held little in the way of a promising future for me. Once word got around that the railroad was not going to continue through to the town, and the panic of 1873 had already taken its toll, money grew tighter and harder to find, and I thought it time to leave Texas entirely and travel on to Colorado.

I left town for Denver, returning to Dallas one last time, where, on a Tuesday morning, April 13, 1875, I went down to the county courthouse and pled guilty to a charge of gaming. A jury of twelve good and lawful men considered the evidence before them. The foreman, who went by the name of McDowell, read the verdict: "We the jury in a plea of guilty assess the punishment as a fine of $10." I paid the damned thing and thereby avoided having to wait around town for the trial, and I boarded a coach of the El Paso Stage Line to begin my trip north to Colorado's mile-high city. I was so happy to leave the state of Texas that I hadn't even taken the opportunity to close out my affairs in Denison.

The stage carried me nearly 160 miles west through Fort Worth, Weatherford, Jackson Borough, and Fort Belknap to the Texas town of Fort Griffin, in northwestern Shackelford County. Before continuing on to Denver, I decided to take a brief walk around town, stretch my legs, and see why this wretched little place was quickly gaining a reputation as one of the most notorious places in the West. Fort Griffin had originally been constructed to house the four companies of the Sixth Cavalry and three companies of the Seventeenth infantry regiments garrisoned there. The fort had grown into the largest government post in the western half of the state. The town's location on the new cattle trail placed it at the center of a forging and dynamic young industry. By the end of the Red River War in the spring of 1875, in which the Kiawah, Comanche, and Southern Cheyenne had been defeated, "the flat," which is the nickname the town had earned for itself, boasted more than a thousand full-time residents, with twice that number of transient hunters and cowboys descending upon Fort Griffin at least once yearly. Their presence, though rowdy at times, was generally welcomed, since they brought with them the money that was so necessary to fuel the engine of commerce. Drifters, gamblers, and prostitutes combined to give the town its reputation as one of the wildest on the Texas frontier.

One of the first places I visited in Fort Griffin was a small bar called the Beehive. It was a two-room adobe building at the northern end of town fronting on Griffin Avenue, the town's main street. One of the two partners running the saloon was my old friend Owen Donnelly, the brother-in-law of the notorious scallywag John Selman. Donnelly had recently arrived in Fort Griffin from Dallas, where he had kept a boarding house and saloon. He opened the Beehive along with his partner, Patrick Carroll, a nice-enough-looking man. It had a dance hall in the rear and several gaming tables in the front, lending it an aura of superficial respectability.

After settling in for a round of gambling, I once again found myself on the wrong side of the law. On June 12, 1875, Sheriff Henry Jacobs arrested me and another gambler, a fellow by the name of Mike Lynch, for "playing together and with each other at a game of cards in a house in which spirituous liquors were sold," a violation of both Texas state law and the Shackelford County anti-gambling ordinance. What a surprise. Lynch had been indicted on the same charge only four weeks earlier. Although such indictments were commonplace in Texas, serving as a means of raising income for the town, I realized it was entirely possible that the city fathers were trying to send a message to Doc Holliday: *Get out while the getting's good.*

As I was not anxious for any new legal entanglements at this point in my life, I did as was desired and promptly left Fort Griffin, failing this time even to take the opportunity to clear up the minor charge still pending against me.

Not one to wear out my welcome, I boarded the stage headed for Fort Concho, realizing that my lifestyle over the past two years had not been exactly conducive to my therapeutic recuperation. I still had my repressive cough. I still was failing to provide a living at my chosen profession of dentistry (gambling, you understand, I had no choice in selecting; it chose me). I did not know even if my cousin Robert—of whom I had received word had completed his schooling in Philadelphia and anxiously awaited my return—would ever join me in a partnership. I did not know if I would ever be well enough to travel back home to my family in Atlanta. It was a demoralizing thought.

As the stage passed along the old route that had connected the several military posts between forts Worth and El Paso, I had all of these things on my mind. The outposts provided us with protection from the "hostiles," as the locals liked to call them, including both Indians and highwaymen. You could never quite tell which was worse.

Once through El Paso, the stage veered to the north and crossed into new territory, through Las Vegas, New Mexico, and then finally up and over the Dick Wooten Pass into Colorado—first into the sleepy little town of Trinidad and then on to Pueblo and eventually to Colorado Springs before finally coming to a halt in the city of Denver, itself.

Doc Holliday had finally arrived in Colorado.

My Darling Whore

THE KILLING OF ED BAILEY

RECOUNTED BY WYATT EARP

San Francisco Examiner, *August 2, 1896*

Doc Holliday was spending the evening in a poker game, which was his custom whenever the faro bank did not present superior claims on his attention. On his right sat Ed Bailey, who needs no description because he is soon to drop out of this narrative. The trouble began by Ed Bailey monkeying with the deadwood, or what people who live in cities call discards. Doc Holliday admonished him once or twice to "play poker"—which is your seasoned gambler's method of cautioning a friend to stop cheating—but the misguided Bailey persisted in his furtive attentions to the deadwood. Finally, having detected him again, Holliday pulled down a pot without showing his hand, which he had a perfect right to do. Thereupon, Bailey started to throw his gun around on Holliday, as might have been expected. But before he could pull the trigger, Doc Holliday had jerked a knife out of his breast pocket, and with one sideways sweep, had caught Bailey just below the brisket.

I had decided that, since I missed my family so much, I would take some time off to visit my aunt Rebecca Annaleezie Holliday McCoin. She was the younger sister of Henry Holliday and, with her husband Alpheus, had left Georgia in 1872 and moved to Kansas City. When I arrived my aunt went on about what a fine young man I had become. She hadn't seen me since my return to Atlanta following my graduation from dental college. I had grown into a very handsome young man, indeed, she said. She must have assumed that the paleness of my cheeks was caused by my tuberculosis. In fact, it was caused more by all the late hours I spent in smoke-filled saloons instead of out in the sunlight, which would most likely have done me more good.

Of course, we had a wealth of family news to discuss. Cousin Robert had graduated from the Pennsylvania College of Dental Surgery, which had led to speculation as to exactly when the two of us would form our partnership. I did not have the heart to tell her that I doubted such an event would ever come to pass. We talked too about Henry Holliday and his recent election to the office of mayor of Valdosta. Uncle Alpheus told me about his experiences as a schoolteacher, and I learned that my beloved cousin Mattie likewise intended to teach school. It was like old times, being with my kin once again, and made me realize just how much I missed and loved them all.

I stayed with my Kansas City relatives for several months until I returned in June 1877 to Denison. By that time I was a different man than I had been two years prior. When I had left Denison the first time, I had realized that my future lay not so much in becoming a successful dental practitioner as it did in becoming a successful sporting man. Since then, I had learned a lot about my newly chosen profession and had become considerably hardened to the ways of the modern-day gambler, as well as to the rigors and the lifestyle of the open frontier.

Following my stay in Denison, I moved on to Breckenridge in Stephens County, Texas. Breckenridge had been founded only a year earlier when the County Court auctioned off a two-hundred-acre parcel of land to establish a trading center for the local residents. The newest of the frontier towns began attracting the sporting crowd almost immediately. I could not resist the temptation to join them, so on Independence Day in 1877, I found myself playing cards at a table with a local gambler by the name of Henry Kahn. After a considerable amount of drinking, Kahn became belligerent, and I warned him to keep his mind on the game. When he called me a cheat and reached for his pistol, I had no alternative but to whack him hard alongside the head with my walking stick. When he went to get up, I struck him again, knocking him down to the floor. Before our quarrel could escalate, both of us had been arrested and hauled off to court, where we each paid our fines for disorderly conduct and were released. Later that day our paths crossed again. This time our renewed argument quickly escalated, and Kahn pulled out a pistol and fired.

Luckily, my adversary was little better a shot than he was a card player, and he inflicted only a minor wound on me. Kahn, as I discovered later, was allegedly on the run from the law, having been indicted in Shackleford County in August on charges of forgery. That in itself, of course, is no reason to deny a man his due. But when he accuses another man of cheating, well . . . I had no alternative, I tell you honestly.

The entire incident might have ended right there, but for a story in the *Dallas Daily Herald* three days later, proclaiming the paper's own take on the matter. "Our reporter was told in Fort Worth yesterday that a young man named Doc Holliday, well known in this city, was shot and killed at Breckenridge last Wednesday by a young man named Kahn." It was the first time, but not the last, that my imminent demise had been sorely misnoted.

When news got out of what had happened, one of my friends telegraphed word of the shooting to my uncle in Atlanta. My family immediately gathered to decide who would come to my aid. I learned later that Uncle John thought he should come because he was a physician, but in the end it was decided that my cousin George would come and see me through my "convalescing."

George Henry Holliday was married at the time to Mary Elizabeth Wright. He and his wife had two young daughters and a son, which must have made the decision to leave for Texas that much more vexing, to say the least. Nevertheless, my cousin boarded the train in Atlanta and traveled west to Breckenridge. He arrived nearly seventeen days after the shooting. Despite the reason for his arrival, I was delighted to see him and placed my recuperation, such that it was, completely in his hands. I had always suspected that the family had sent George not so much to nurse me back to health as to convince me to return home to Atlanta with him. At that he was unsuccessful. When George was finally convinced that I had fully recovered, he returned to Georgia alone, no doubt disappointed that he would be forced to reveal to the entire family my stubborn reluctance to ascend to their wishes.

By that fall, I had completely forgotten about the incident and settled back into my nightly routine. When I was arrested again for gambling in Dallas that September, I decided once again that it was time to move on.

I arrived in Fort Griffin in February 1876, wherein I found a town that had changed remarkably since my last visit. I learned that John M. Larn had been elected sheriff of Shackelford County, succeeding Henry Jacobs, who had been in office when I had last passed through town the year before. Larn had a reputation as a charmer and a ladies' man of many attributes, a gentleman, but also an outlaw, a cow thief, and a killer. He and his deputy, John Henry Selman, had joined with the vigilantes known as the Tin Hat Brigade. They had managed to clean up the countryside of the brigands and outlaws who called the area home. He made little note of the legalities of his actions; and hangings, such as those of Houston Fraught, Charlie McBride, Bill Henderson, and Henry Floyd, to mention only a few, were commonplace.

Larn posted warnings throughout town, advising the ladies of the evening to "leave or you are doomed.—VIGILANCE." The sheriff and his deputy eventually became leaders of the vigilantes, while engaging in the far more profitable activities of stealing cattle and horses on the side. In 1877, after he had secured a contract to supply beef to the Army at Fort Griffin, Larn resigned his position as a lawman, finding it far more lucrative to devote full-time his attentions to his new profession as a cattle inspector, and, of course, a rustler.

In time, the Fort Griffin vigilantes committee was formed to stop the lawlessness. Shackelford County stockmen donned white sheets and became vigilantes themselves, the pot calling the kettle black. As a result, the lynchings multiplied, and the blood continued to flow. Not anxious to unite my allegiances with either side, I determined to stay neutral and concentrate on my gaming. I believe that for once in my young life, I had made the right decision at the appropriate time.

I took up residence in Fort Griffin at the new Planters Hotel, which was run by a very capable hotelier by the name of Jack Schwartz, along with his amenable wife. I settled into a daily routine of playing poker and faro there. And when I was not to be found at the Planters, I was most likely settled into John Shannsey's Cattle Exchange Saloon, located one block to the east. It was there, at "Shanny's," that I made the most precipitous encounter of my life.

Her name was Kate Elder. She was a well-traveled and educated twenty-six-year-old woman of Hungarian extraction. She had been the eldest of seven children born to Michael Harony, a physician, and his second wife, Katharina Baldizar Harony. The family had left Hungary to settle in Davenport, Iowa, in late 1860, shortly after the outbreak of the American Civil War. If this story sounds remotely familiar, it is not by accident. Yes, the two were one-and-the-same.

But I digress. As it turned out, Mary Katherine had taken up residence at Joseph Henry's Theatre Comique at the corner of Fifth and Biddle. She supported herself in a manner most out of keeping with her strict moral Catholic upbringing. She had become a professional woman. She had become a "soiled dove."

In the summer of 1874, Kate had been arrested and fined in Wichita, Kansas, for working in a "sporting house" allegedly run by Sally and Bessie Earp. Undoubtedly, Kate had met the notorious Wyatt Earp while in town. She left the following year and began working as a dance-hall girl in Dodge City, under her newly acquired name of Kate Elder. She said later that she had taken the name because she was the eldest of her four siblings.

By the summer of 1877, Kate Elder had arrived in Fort Griffin, part of the entourage of James and Bessie Earp. She immediately caught my eye, the twinkle that I had known only once before in a woman and admired so. I had until that time met many worldly ladies since leaving Dallas. Kate was more than refreshing. She was very near my intellectual equal, a stimulating companion with a strong, wild independent streak in her, just begging to be tamed. She was beautiful, hair the color of golden sunshine, eyes that sparkled like prairie-grass dew. Her nose, contrary to popular opinion, was not overly large. It was rather more Romanesque, more in keeping with the classic Roman tradition and the noses of all great European dignitaries. Far from dainty, it leant her an air of Continental sophistication. How could I possibly resist such pulchritude?

In me, I suppose, Kate had found a rarely intelligent man, with impeccable manners and proper upbringing. I stood out in marked contrast to the rough, raucous, crude men who filled to overflowing all western cattle towns. Although she never admitted it, she must have seen within me something that led her to believe that I could accept freely the manner in which she had chosen to make her living. She was right, of course. Just as she was right in recognizing how often I had deviated from the lessons of my own youth. We were meant for each other, this soiled dove and I. And we spent a good deal of our time together in Shannsey's, where Kate soon took to accompanying me when I set up shop at the faro table in the evenings.

It wasn't long, predictably, before our relationship grew into something more than a congenial friendship, and we became a pair, widely recognized as shacking up together. I remember our first time quite vividly. She had come to my room at the Planters under some pretext, and before I knew what had happened, we had each downed a couple of bourbons and branch, and as I lay in bed watching her eyes sparkling in the candlelight, I saw in her something childlike, vulnerable, and yet as wild and deadly as anything I had ever known before in my life. I knew right then and there that I had met my match.

Of course, Kate and I enjoyed our time together, feeding off each other, propping one another up. Whenever I got an attack, a coughing fit, often in the middle of the night, she would be there for me, to comfort me, hold me, stroke my temple, pour me a drink. And whenever she got into trouble, with a tough or someone who thought he should not have to pay for what he was used to getting for free back east, I was there, watching her back. More than one rowdy slipped away from her when I stood before him, showing him down. I think, had it come right to it, I might even have drawn on such a cur and sent him to his wings, had the opportunity so presented itself. Fortunately for me, it did not.

But as good as things were between Kate and me, we were not what I would call a match made in heaven. Not even for a Methodist. No, she had her own life to live, which I fully understood, and I had mine. So whenever we could manage to play a role in each other's affairs, we would do so; and the other times, we would each of us go our separate ways.

That was another thing I liked about her.

Don't get me wrong. It is not that I would not have killed for a woman to worship and adore, to admire and respect and to love, a woman of substance and an infinite capacity for caring. A woman such as my own departed mother. Or my cousin, Mattie.

Oh, yes, I would have liked that more than anything. But in my line of work—constantly traveling around, following the rails just over the next horizon—and with the state of my health being in such a tear, I doubted that a relationship with such a woman was anywhere near to my future. At least not so I could tell.

So I found myself—with a certain amount of mixed emotions—at first drawing near to Kate and at the same time pulling back, inserting a fair amount of distance between us, not in the hopes of sparing me my feelings, but rather in sparing her hers.

I do admit to feeling pangs of devil jealousy from time to time when while wrapped in the business of counting cards, I would spy her from the corner of my eye coming on to a dandy. The toughs, I never worried about; for I knew she was only playing them for a song. But a gentleman—well, he was another matter. Kate fancied herself a genteel woman; and she would have been, too, had circumstances and the cards dealt to her early in life played out differently. But as it was, she was just young enough and impressionable enough to be lured by some well-heeled stud into letting her guard down.

Of course, I soon enough learned that she, too, had an Achilles' heel. Most notably, one who went by the name of Lottie Deno.

A woman of some breeding and character, much as my beloved Kate, Lottie came to Fort Griffin sometime around spring of 1877. She was mysterious, well mannered, and attractive, with fiery red hair, which made her an instantly likeable fixture in the saloons around town. Lottie—whose real name was Carlotte Tompkins—was a whore who soon enough managed to obtain part ownership of the Gus, a local saloon and boarding house, where she built a reputation as "the poker queen" because of her undeniable skill at both poker and faro.

When I first met Lottie at the tables, I knew little about her except from what tall tales the locals had managed to whittle together. She is said to have followed a former Georgian by the name of Frank Thurmond to Griffin. Thurmond was another San Antonio gambler on the run. Using the alias of Mike Fogarty, Thurmond found odd jobs—either he worked as a bartender at the Beehive or he ran some cattle, or he worked now and again as a shotgun on stagecoaches.

Lottie is said to have been involved, too, with a gambler by the name of Johnny Golden, but Golden had been killed by Marshal Bill Gilson in July before I had returned to Fort Griffin, so I could not personally attest to that fact. By the time I had come to town, Lottie had grown to be increasingly reclusive, although she continued to support herself at the tables. I checked in to the Occidental Hotel and opened an account at Smith's bar on September 14. Within a week I had managed to run up a tab of just over $20 for my room and board, $50 in gambling debts, and a little more than $120 for liquor. Let no one accuse me of failing to recognize my priorities. Naturally, much of that liquor was consumed at the faro table, for I realized that I had a rather high capacity for spirituous libations, and I found that I could drink nearly any man—or woman—quickly under the table. Lottie was damned near the only exception. She was as good with her cards as she was with her bourbon. A man by the name of John Jacobs is credited with having told this story, to which I ascribe its veracity:

> In your recent letter, you asked if faro was a popular game at old Fort Griffin. It certainly was popular; every gambling house there had a faro bank. I remember well one instance where a lot of money changed hands, and Lottie Deno coming about $3,000 ahead, winning it all from Doc Holliday at the Beehive. It seems that Holliday had won 3,000 dollars and the layout from Mike Fogarty [*sic*], who operated the gambling resort, when Lottie Deno, who was lookout for Fogarty, proposed to Holliday that she be given a chance to recoup Fogarty's losses. Holliday agreed to this, and the game was resumed with a $50 limit. The game did not last very long, for Lottie Deno copped every bet, and left Doc Holliday completely strapped for the time being at least, for he was not one who let poor luck get him down and keep him there. He got into a poker game the next night and won $500 and a diamond ring from an Army officer stationed at the Fort.

Of course, Kate, like any self-respecting woman, grew increasingly jealous of Lottie, and one night, after having had a little too much to drink, accused her of trying to steal her man. Lottie sprang to her feet and shouted something to the effect of, "Why you low-down slinking slut! If I should step in soft cow manure, I would not even clean my boot on that bastard. I'll show you a thing or two!" Both Lottie and Kate drew weapons, and for a moment I feared that bloodshed was imminent. I grabbed Kate by the arm and held my hat out to Lottie before bowing. Still clutching the wildcat in my grasp, I told them how honored I was to be the subject of a fight between two such beautiful ladies of the evening, and Lottie spat on the floor before turning and heading once more for the bar.

As I moved my attentions onto my ubiquitous whore, she yanked her arm free and, stuffing her pistol back into her petticoat, said, "You should have let me kill her, Doc. That's all I was aiming to do."

I smiled, picked up my glass from the table, and drained the liquid dry. "Why, darlin'," I said, "I could not allow you to do any such thing. She still has my $3,000."

Si verum exsisto notus: If truth be known.

Later that fall Wyatt and Mattie Earp arrived in Fort Griffin. Wyatt had dropped into the saloon to see his old friend from Cheyenne, John Shannsey who, like Wyatt, was a former pugilist. After several minutes of reliving golden moments in the ring, Shannsey brought the lawman over to our table, where, he announced with some degree of certainty, he said he expected to find the both of us more often than not in the weeks to come. Shannsey left us to our own, and we talked a little about gambling, about our pasts, about Dodge City. Wyatt asked about Kate, and I told him of her near-fatal run-in with Lottie Deno. "Be careful of her," the lawman said. "She's a cobra. She'll bite you if you're not looking."

"Why, Wyatt," I said, squinting up at him as if we'd been standing outside in the bright Texas sun. "You sound like an old jealous hag. Surely you can't mean her so."

Wyatt laughed, and I held up my glass for a refill. And then I asked Wyatt about his days of boxing, and he asked me about my life of dentistry, and then our talk turned to Kansas. Wyatt insisted that he was heading out that way, and I asked him everything I could possibly think to ask about the place. I found the man to be quite congenial and, if a little rough around the edges from his years as a plainsman, pleasant enough nonetheless. He made Dodge City sound so enticing that I could not fight off the notion that I might want to see it myself someday. And that I might want to see it someday when Wyatt was there to show me around.

Little did I realize at the time, but my thoughts were about to become reality.

A short while later I found myself spending the evening playing poker with Ed Bailey, a braggart and a local lout whom nobody in particular seemed to like. Bailey, sitting to my right, kept monkeying with the deadwood. I warned him—as you have already by now surely heard from the testimony of my good friend Wyatt Earp—but to no avail.

Now, Wyatt was a good and an honorable man. Although he lived to tell the story of my confrontation with that blackguard and spurious scallywag Bailey, he was not there when it all transpired.

It is true that Bailey and I ended up alone that evening, in that all other players had dropped out of the game. And it is likewise true that Bailey, who was drunk and obnoxious and in general an extremely vexatious man, kept picking up my deadwood to see what kinds of cards I had been holding, and perhaps to test my mettle.

The first time it happened, I motioned for the bar girl to bring me another bourbon and branch and, when she arrived, I turned back to face Bailey, urging him to quit monkeying with the cards and play poker.

Bailey belched something that for him, I have no doubt, was emblematic of the epitome of intellectual prowess. And when, after completing the next hand, he reached across the table and once again picked up my discards, I warned him a second time.

In the next hand, I had placed my bet on the strength of a baby straight and called, and Bailey laid out his hand on the table. Quite calmly and deliberately, I folded my own cards and placed them face-down well out of reach of the oaf and proceeded to rake in the winnings.

"Hey!" Bailey shouted. "What are you doing? You didn't show me your cards."

"Ed Bailey, you are a cur and a scoundrel, unworthy of response," I said casually. "You have been warned about cheating twice, and I am through wasting my breath on a pestiferous blackguard such as yourself."

For some reason, the man took offense to my words and reached suddenly below the table to withdraw his piece, which he aimed directly at my head before reaching his thumb for the hammer. Within an instant I had pulled my long knife and lunged at him, shoving the dagger to the hilt into his brisket, just below his heart.

Naturally, that ended the game.

Unfortunately, while the proprietor attempted to clean the blood from the table and the floor around the body, some misguided soul had summoned the local law, who, upon learning my identity, proceeded to place me under arrest, the town having no properly installed jail as of yet, into my room at the hotel, where he set two armed constables outside my door. I was told that I was being held pending investigation of the killing of Ed Bailey.

The crowd outside the hotel, growing larger and angrier by the moment at the brash state of affairs transpiring in their own backyard, had awakened my beloved Kate, who was in her room just down the street from the scene. I had not lived in Fort Griffin very long, and Ed Bailey, although vexatious, was nonetheless well tolerated. The townspeople reacted as anyone would to an outsider coming into their midst and killing one of their own, when in all actuality they might rather have presented me a medal.

While the crowd continued to clamor for my blood, tainted as it may have been, I looked out the back window and spied Kate. She waved at me quickly, and then she disappeared down the alleyway, which I thought at the time to be an unlikely thing to do. Later, after reuniting with her, I learned that what she had heard and seen led her to believe that my life was not worth ten minutes' purchase, and I believe in retrospect that she may have been correct.

As I sat on the bed, wondering about my general well-being and speculating upon my opportunities for longevity, I heard a new ruckus well up from the crowd outside the hotel. Someone shouted "Fire," and the next time I looked out, everyone was running down the alleyway toward a bright orange glow in the sky just above the horizon. Kate, my beloved darling, had found a shed at the back of the lot and, after freeing a single mare bridled there, set fire to the building and began calling out.

It all transpired just as she had planned it. The shed blazed up, and she hammered at the door, yelling at the top of her lungs. Everybody rushed out, except the marshal, the constables, and their prisoner. But the two guards left their post outside my door long enough to descend to the hotel lobby in order to see what was happening, providing me the opportunity to sneak down behind them just as Kate, who had borrowed a pistol from a friend, which, when added to the one she always carried, gave her two, walked through the doors. She drew one of her six-shooters on the marshal and handed the other to me.

"Come on, Doc," she laughed, no doubt finding the sight of three experienced lawmen with their hands high over their heads amusing.

I needed no second invitation.

We backed our way out of the hotel, keeping our pistols trained on the officers, and worked ourselves on foot down to the willows along the creek, where we huddled until daybreak. One of Kate's friends brought us horses and some of the clothes from my room the next morning, and Kate dressed up quite handsomely in a pair of pants, some boots, a shirt, and a hat, so that, to anyone at first glance, we would have looked like two drifters making our way out of town. I knew instinctively where we were heading next. As the two of us followed the Rath Trail, which was used to move pioneers through the buffalo lands, we headed north toward Sweetwater, stopping only long enough along the way for me to send off a letter to my cousin Martha Anne.

"[I] enjoyed about as much of this [Texas] as [I] could stand."

We rode the four hundred miles to Dodge City, where we took a room and awaited the return home of Wyatt Earp, which transpired the following May.

When Wyatt inquired as to our luck at the gaming tables in Fort Griffin, I informed him that Kate and I had cleaned out the town. He looked at me mischievously and grinned, and I smiled back, recalling a good piece of advice he had once shared with me. Never tell a lawman more than he needs to know.

Vendetta's Edge

THE KILLING OF MIKE GORDON

Las Vegas Daily Gazette, *July 26, 1879*

Gordon was standing in the street to the right of the hall after some of his threats and drew a revolver and fired, the bullet passing through the pants leg of a Mexican and struck in the floor in line with the bartender who was standing at the rear of the bar.

Other shots were fired immediately but it is difficult to tell how or by whom.

It is said that Gordon fired a second shot. Every person there says three shots were fired, while several maintain that five in all were fired.

Gordon at once ceased firing and disappeared. An hour or two later a Mr. Kennedy went into his tent some thirty or forty yards away, to go to bed and hearing groans investigated and found Gordon laying on the ground outside. The news soon spread and his woman arriving on the ground had him taken to her room east of the Court house, where he died at 6 o'clock Sunday morning. In the afternoon the Coroner held an inquest and the jury returned a verdict of excusable homicide.

Dodge City had been built from the ground up in 1872. Before that, it had been little more than a wide spot in the road where traders met occasionally to swap yarns and whatever goods they could bring to the table. It was situated in the heart of Buffalo country, which meant its main source of income was serving the needs of the hunters. But when the railroad arrived later that year, the town found a new way to generate income. Texas cattlemen in need of a manner by which to move their herds from southwestern Texas found it at the loading grounds just west of the city. The growth of the cattle industry boomed to the point where, by 1878, some 260,000 head of longhorn, accompanied by 1,300 rowdy Texas cowboys, drove into town. The average drover earned around $30 for each month on the trail. By the time they hit Dodge, they had built up a tidy sum of cash, and they were anxious as hell to spend it.

The cowboys sought out food, whiskey, women, and the excitement awaiting them at the gaming tables. Always on the alert for new opportunities, I succumbed to the lure that the drovers extended to me. Kate and I, faced with the necessity of leaving Fort Griffin in somewhat of a hurry, arrived in Dodge in the spring of 1878. We took a room at the Dodge House, which was generally regarded as the finest hotel in town. It boasted fifty rooms, a restaurant, a bar, and the best damned billiard parlor in the West. It also had a first-class laundry, which was important to me since I enjoyed dressing immaculately. Each day Kate would put out a freshly laundered, starched, and ironed shirt. I would punctuate my appearance with a cravat held in place by my diamond stickpin and finished off by a gray overcoat.

Dodge City at the time of our arrival was something of a misnomer. It was not a city by any means. It was a megalopolis. It was the purest definition of the West—a gateway to history that began with the opening of the Santa Fe Trail by William Becknell in 1821. The Santa Fe, sometimes called simply "the Trail," had become the most popular of commercial routes spanning the map between Franklin, Missouri, and Santa Fe, New Mexico. Several thousand wagons traveled the so-called Mountain Branch of the trail, which wound its way west from Dodge along the north bank of the Arkansas River into the high country of Colorado. For those hardier souls willing to risk the pitfalls of waterless sand hills and parching heat, a shorter route called the Cimarron Cutoff crossed near Dodge and traveled southwest to the river of the same name. God forbid those who took it.

Fort Dodge had been established by the end of the Civil War near the present site of the city in order to protect wagon trains, the U.S. Mail Service, and hunters from Indians and the local brigands. It served, too, as a supply base for troops engaged in the Indian Wars. Kiowa, Cheyenne, and other plains tribes inhabited the surrounding lands, where wild game—including vast herds of roaming bison—was abundant.

Dodge City itself got its start in 1871, when a rancher by the name of Henry L. Sitler built a three-room sod-roof house five miles east of the fort at the foot of a hill along the Trail. He built it to oversee his cattle ranch, but it soon became a regular stopover for buffalo hunters and traders.

By September 1872 the glimmering steel rails of the newly arrived Atchison, Topeka and Santa Fe unfurled their hardened banners just south of town. By then, hastily constructed frame buildings and tents had popped up to reveal a couple of grocery stores, a general merchandise emporium, a dance hall, a restaurant, a barber shop, a blacksmith shop, and even a saloon—right next to Sitler's original home. The famous Front Street legend was born. And Dodge City was breaking all records for new growth.

Stacks of bison hides—buffalo, we called them—mounded up along Front Street, the stench from the filthy men who made a living hunting and skinning them mounding up along with them. That's where the term "stinker" was coined.

Much less objectionable to the nose, the trainmasters would pull into town and, on their layovers, carry their swinging red caboose lanterns with them when they went to call upon the town's ladies of the night. And the term "red-light district" was born.

All in all, it was an amazing time to be alive, and an amazing place in which to be so. Yet it was not without its pitfalls. During those early years, Dodge City acquired its infamous reputation for wild lawlessness and vile gunslingers. There existed little to no local law enforcement, and the military at the fort lacked jurisdiction over the townspeople. Buffalo hunters, railroad workers, drifters, and soldiers scrapped and fought twenty-four hours a day, leading to spur-of-the-moment shootings where men literally died with their boots on. So many men died, in fact, that a special burial place was created to hold them. They called it Boot Hill.

Back then the cemetery was on the outskirts of town. Today it's an integral part of the city. Before Boot Hill, the deceased who had friends or money or enough political clout within the community were buried in the military post cemetery at the fort. The others came to rest wherever digging a hole proved convenient.

Dodge City had been the buffalo capital of the universe for three years until their mass slaughter destroyed the huge herds and left the prairie littered with decaying carcasses. It was an unfortunate side effect of the railroads' push west. The workers had to eat, and the food supply at first appeared inexhaustible. More than three-quarters of a million of the animals were slain between 1872 and 1874, their hides shipped east from Dodge for manufacturing into coats and boots and shoes and whatever else an inventive mind could conceive. Farmers, during hard times, gathered the buffalo bones and rendered them into soup or glue, and then they sold what remained for $6 to $8 a ton to use in the manufacture of china and fertilizer.

But like all good things, the herds soon dried up, and the buffalo were gone as a source of revenue by 1875. Fortunately for the town, the even more lucrative business of cattle was only beginning. A new boom was born.

Drovers began driving their longhorns out of west Texas as soon as they learned of the railroad's arrival in Dodge. But they drove more than cattle. They drove dollars and industry and boom times and legends. Hell, for the next decade, they drove more than five million head up over the lands where the buffalo once roamed, up and over and onto the grazing lands outside of the city proper, where they rested and fattened up until being herded onboard the planks heading east to feed a hungry nation. They came up the western branch of the Chisholm and Western Trails to Dodge, and they were loaded into crowded boxcars and shipped out. It was an industry like no other in American history. I swear to God. And like the slaughter of the buffalo, the movement through Dodge of the Texas longhorns seemed an inexhaustible supply of cash.

Of course, where there is money, there are people willing to spend it. And where those people congregate, there are people willing to help them to do just that. Which is, of course, what brought me to the new gateway to the West in the first place. Me and respectable law officers in search of work, men such as Bat Masterson, Wyatt Earp, Bill Tilghman, and Charlie Bassett. The town that they were charged with controlling boasted two Front Streets—one north of the tracks and one south. The city fathers, in their endless exhibition of labored thoughtfulness, banned the possession of weapons north of the tracks, called the "deadline." South of the tracks, on the other hand, anything went. And I mean *anything*.

Gambling ran rampant, of course. Give a bored and saddle-sore cowboy a pocketful of spending money, and once he's had himself a woman, a hot meal, and a couple of drinks, it was the only game in town. Gaming around the time I arrived in Dodge ranged from 5-cent "Chuck-a-Luck" to thousand-dollar poker pots. A lot of gambling halls offered musical entertainment, whether a piano player, a singer, or, as Chalk Beeson did in his Long Branch Saloon, a full five-piece musical ensemble. Beeson also founded and played in the notorious Cowboy Band, which traveled throughout the West, appearing at cattlemen's conventions, concerts, soirees, and even in Washington, D.C., at the inauguration of President Benjamin Harrison in 1890.

I was a little surprised when arriving in town to discover three medical doctors already settled in there, one of whom was actually licensed. Dr. Thomas McCarty was also the town coroner, one of its founding fathers, and a leading apostolate of the newly arrived Roman Catholic Church. One of the other doctors actually worked more on animals than on people. All three of them practiced dentistry. With my arrival, the town suddenly found itself with *two* licensed medical practitioners. Both Thom McCarty and I had gone to school in Philadelphia. McCarty, at twenty-nine, was two years my senior, and we hit things off fairly well—so much so that he felt secure enough with my medical skills to recommend me freely to his patients. I never did have the feeling that he much enjoyed rooting around in people's mouths.

So I set up shop at the Dodge House, where in fact I spent nearly all of my time, practicing dentistry by day and playing cards by night.

Surprisingly, many of my best gaming customers were the lawmen in town who ended up in the saloons after hours, every bit as anxious as everybody else to kill some free time and take a chance at scoring big. It was at the hotel where I met the Masterson brothers, Ed, Bat, and Jim. Ed at the time was marshal of Dodge, while Bat had taken a job as sheriff of Ford County.

When Ed was shot down by two mangy curs by the name of Jack Wagner and Alf Walker, Charles E. Bassett took the job. Shortly after Ed's assassination, Wyatt and Mattie returned to town, and on May 12, 1878, Wyatt took the position as Bassett's assistant.

In those days, a lawman's pay was so meager that he often had to supplement his income by being a house dealer or a faro banker. A lawman's position of authority in the town lent him an air of integrity that was seldom questioned and even more seldom earned.

Most of the sporting houses in Dodge were located along Front Street north of the plaza and south of Dodge City's railroad tracks, just across from the cattle-holding area. They were the first buildings the cowboys saw as they rode in. You understand, of course, that these buildings were the saloons and dance halls and brothels—what else?

Despite my growing friendship with the various lawmen who called Dodge home—or perhaps because of it—I was able to avoid any serious ruckuses with the law during my tenure there. If anything, my close associations gave me a feeling of some pride in being viewed by the locals as a shirttail lawman. Andy Adams, a drover from Texas, once wrote that "the roster of peace officials of Dodge City . . . during the brief span of the trail days, were the brothers, Ed, Jim, and 'Bat' Masterson, Wyatt Earp, Jack Bridges, 'Doc' Holliday, Charles Bassett, William Tillman [*sic*], 'Shotgun' Collins, Mayor A. B. Webster, and 'Mysterious' Dave Mather."

True, I was not a lawman by any legal sense of the word, but I never took a step to correct the notion, which I always felt lent me an air of respectability as well—something few other sporting men in town could say.

As summer crept upon us, I decided to stay awhile longer than Kate and I had originally planned in order to capitalize on the cowboys who were already within striking distance of home. So, on June 28 the *Dodge City Times* carried the announcement:

"DENTISTRY. J. H. Holliday, Dentist, very respectfully offers his professional services to the citizens of Dodge City and surrounding county during the summer. Office at Room No. 24, Dodge House. Where satisfaction is not given money will be refunded."

It paid off. At least it did in one sense. For the next several months, I kept up my dual lifestyle, practicing dentistry during the day and drinking, carousing, and gambling at night. My medical practice gave me an additional air of respectability at the tables, just as it provided me with the stakes any sporting man must have in order to be successful in his profession.

Perhaps I should have used more discretion in my choice of activities, I came to realize, for my consumption grew steadily worse. Those long nights in those smoke-filled rooms did me little good. I found myself losing weight, mostly because when I began to cough heavily, I drank to overcome the constant shooting pain. And when I drank I lost my appetite for food. But the temptation of playing cards in order to separate the oafs and louts pouring steadily into the city from their money proved too lucrative a prospect to ignore. To tell you the truth, I'm not sure I would have spent all that much more time tending to my dentistry practice even if I hadn't been suffering from consumption. There is something awfully appealing about oafs and louts.

Not all gamblers fit that description, of course. Bat Masterson was a more temperate and educated gamesman, as was Wyatt Earp, who had quickly become one of my favorite people in town. Wyatt always treated me with great respect and civility, although he had no rational reason for doing so. So when I had an opportunity to return the favor, I exercised it gladly.

Wyatt recalled the story while testifying under oath in Tombstone, Arizona Territory, sometime later: "I am a friend of Doc Holliday because when I was city marshal of Dodge City, Kansas, he came to my rescue and saved my life when I was surrounded by desperadoes."

A reporter added to Wyatt's commentary from an interview he had done earlier. He quoted Wyatt as saying, "Doc saw a man draw on me from behind my back. 'Look out, Wyatt!' he shouted, but while the words were coming out of his mouth he had jerked his pistol out of his pocket and shot the other fellow before the latter could fire."

I have viewed with more than a little amusement over the years other tales of that incident grown completely out of proportion, but nonetheless it is nice to know that Wyatt had always appreciated my efforts on his behalf, no matter how meager they may in reality have been. Wyatt had always credited me with saving his life. The truth of the matter is that I may have done just that. The truth of the matter is that it doesn't matter. Wyatt had become my friend, my brother away from home, and I would have done whatever in my power to spare him any indignity.

But that wasn't enough to stave the fall. By the latter months of 1878, my health had deteriorated to the point where I could barely get up mornings. Kate and I decided it might be best to leave Dodge City and head west to Las Vegas, New Mexico Territory, along the Santa Fe Trail. Las Vegas was well known and highly regarded as a haven for people with tuberculosis. I realized that if I could pursue my practice of dentistry and avoid the gaming tables late into the night, if I could somehow manage to focus my intents upon the advantages of the town's healthful sulfur-laden hot springs, I could cure myself. I promised as much to Kate, who increasingly expressed her concerns over my overall lack of well-being.

By the time we had traveled from Dodge City to Trinidad, Colorado, my consumption had only worsened. I told Kate in Trinidad that I did not think I could complete the trip by horseback. I told her that I was feeling the way my own mother had felt and looked and sounded so many years ago, just before she died. I told her that I was prepared to die then and there and that she should go on without me. She chastised me soundly, calling me an old frightened lady, and saying that she was embarrassed to hear me speak so. She would remain with me until we could both travel to New Mexico. Kate later wrote in her diary, "Then we had to hire an outfit to take us [the rest of the way] to Las Vegas, New Mexico. We traveled with a big freight outfit."

We did indeed manage to join a freight train, traveling as Dr. and Mrs. John H. Holliday, in order to spare Kate any possible indignities in what was going to become our new home, and began the grueling trek up and over the pass between southern Colorado and northern New Mexico just in time to greet the winter's snows. By the time we had descended into Raton and forged forward another hundred miles to Las Vegas, it was a few days before Christmas, 1878. The town was abuzz with news of the arrival of the Santa Fe, scheduled to occur within six months, and I could not have been happier. The fates had smiled upon me once again. My consumption had taken a sudden turn for the better, briefly—do not ask me why, except that it was as if the clearing of my lungs of the tainted Arizona air and its replacement with the drier, clearer, cleaner air of the southern Rockies plateau had breathed new life into them, and me.

Las Vegas, New Mexico Territory, had as its primary attraction besides several hundred Mexicans who called the area home its hot springs—twenty-two of them, to be exact, located at the foot of the mountains and producing bubbling, spewing waters that ranged from 110 to 140 degrees F. I came to see for myself the wonders of these miracle springs and met upon the occasion several wealthy young tuberculars who had come to Las Vegas from all corners of the nation, seeking a cure for their disease. A number of them chose to make the area home, and they formed what they called the Lungers' Club.

After the first night of taking the vapors, Kate and I emerged and, toweling off, loaded ourselves into a livery buggy for the drive back to town. The very next day, Kate set out to find employment while I perused the local newspaper for locations for my new dental practice. I found a fair enough spot on the north side of Bridge Street near the Plaza and set about turning the space into a professional office. The timing could not have been worse.

New Mexico was experiencing its coldest winter in memory, the snows flying as far south as Albuquerque and beyond, with record snowfalls and temperatures plunging to below zero. The locals squirreled away in their adobe and log homes, the fires kept burning through the most frigid of times. Kate and I stayed at the hotel, of course; and when I did venture out, it was only to be met by the blank stare of prosperity on the run. The dentistry business was less than brisk.

About the same time, the New Mexico territorial legislature, in its infinite wisdom, sought to pass legislation that would prohibit gambling within the territory. Nobody expected it to pass, of course. But "nobody" was mistaken. On Saturday, March 8, 1879, I was indicted under the new statute for "keeping [a] gaming table." On March 10, I pleaded guilty and paid a $25 fine, plus court costs of $1.75.

As spring threatened to descend upon the town, I realized that the cold, harsh winter had done me more harm than good, both physically and financially. I took Kate to one side and told her that I thought it would be best for my health to catch a stage for Otero, and then the railroad back to Dodge City, where I could convalesce. I asked her if she would accompany me, and she said that she would prefer to remain behind. At least for the time being.

I had rather much anticipated that response, since our relationship at the time had been somewhat strained. Vengeful, actually. So, with that settled, I made good my pledge and returned to Kansas, where I was met by Bat Masterson, who had taken a job working as a United States marshal protecting the Santa Fe Railroad from rival gangs.

The Santa Fe was attempting to construct a route from Canyon City through the Royal Gorge to the silver-rich town of Leadville,

Colorado. But the Denver and Rio Grande Railroad claimed the same rich route. The Royal Gorge War, which had been fought in the courts for months, was about ready to spill over into the streets.

On March 23 Masterson hastily assembled a ragtag posse of thirty-three men, "armed to the teeth." We boarded the Santa Fe for Pueblo, which was the hub of the Santa Fe Road. Among those joining us was Texas gunman Ben Thompson, whose reputation as a cold-blooded killer was well earned. I remember trying to persuade my old friend Eddie Foy to take a break from his performances in Dodge and join us on our mission. Foy asked me why on earth I thought he would be of any use to us, and I told him that every man carrying a gun would be one more advantage for our side. Besides, I said, the railroad had promised good pay for the fighters.

"But listen, Mr. Holliday," Foy said, "I'm no fighter. I wouldn't be any help to the gang. I couldn't hit a man if I shot him."

That didn't matter, I told him. The Santa Fe would never know the difference. "Just come on along and collect your pay. You can use a shotgun if you want to."

In the end Foy turned down the invitation, so Bat and his posse got off the train at Pueblo, a hundred miles or so to the south of Denver, where we remained holed up for nearly three months. In time we barricaded ourselves in the Santa Fe Roundhouse. That did not go over well with the founder of the Denver and Rio Grande, which organized its own armed party and enlisted the assistance of the local County Sheriff's office and even brought in Company B of the Colorado First Cavalry. Damn. It was the Civil War all over again.

And then, one afternoon, around three o'clock on June 11, the Pueblo County Sheriff and 150 deputized locals showed up and demanded that we surrender. I turned to Masterson and asked what he wanted to do. He told me to remain behind while he went to talk to the others, waiting outside. I told him I thought we should shoot our way past the sons of bitches. He said to wait. When he came back in, he showed me a roll of hundred-dollar bills paid by the Denver and Rio Grande for us to leave peacefully. I pocketed my share of the $10,000 and boarded the train back for Otero, followed by the stage for the hundred-mile run back to Las Vegas and Kate. I was hoping that the new gaming legislation had by then been overturned and that I could reestablish my dental practice and reunite with my own little dove.

But the Las Vegas to which I returned was not the one that I had left several months earlier. Although I enjoyed a short period of rest and recuperation with my fellow lungers at the Hot Springs, it was not to last.

When the Santa Fe finally arrived in town on July 4, 1879, it carried along with it a number of luminaries and numerous members of the sporting element from Kansas and Colorado, who followed the railroads on their way to prosperity that lay just over the next knoll. Among these sporting men were several people I had befriended in Dodge, including Hoodoo Brown, a onetime buffalo hunter and saloonkeeper; Dave Rudabaugh; Mysterious Dave Mather; Dutch Henry; and John Webb.

When the final tracks had finally been laid, the townsfolk were disheartened to learn that the railroad had bypassed Main Street by a country mile. There was all kinds of talk about legal suits and such before the residents came to their senses and quickly set about throwing up tents and slapping together hastily constructed clapboard buildings to try to capture some of the benefits of what was sure to be a lucrative new commercial hub. Almost overnight an entirely new town sprang up, full of restaurants and saloons, gaming parlors and brothels, all ready to cater to the desires of the newcomers to town. The townsfolk named this new mini-city East Las Vegas, but most everybody called it New Town.

Not surprisingly, the law had not managed to keep pace with the new growth, and lawlessness and killings reigned. On July 19, 1879, according to a report in the local *Las Cruces Thirty-Four,* "Mike Gordon got drunk at a dance hall in Vegas and began a bluff by drawing a pair of sixes and firing promiscuously around the room. Some unknown person called the hand, and Gordon was froze out. He was buried at the expense of the county the next day. Vegas is a bad town to bluff."

That's what the story had said. In reality Gordon had been drinking heavily when he entered the dance hall on Centre Street. He grabbed his girl and ordered her to leave with him. When she refused he stormed out, and everybody pretty much thought that was that. But a short while later, Gordon came back and began firing randomly, some shots going in the direction of the dance hall, others every which way. A few hours later a badly wounded Mike Gordon was found forty yards away. He died before sunup.

Predictably, nobody could—or, more likely, *would*—identify the shooter who killed Gordon before Gordon could kill someone else. A coroner's jury was empowered to look into the matter and returned a verdict of excusable homicide by a person unknown.

Bat Masterson had a different take on the subject, however, when he gave an interview to the *Las Vegas Daily Optic* several years later. "About an hour afterward, though, Gordon came back and fired a shot from the side-walk into the saloon. The bullet whizzed a couple of inches from Holliday's head and went crashing through a window at the rear of the room. 'Doc' drew his gun and rushed to the front door and saw Gordon standing on the sidewalk with a revolver in his hand. Gordon raised his revolver to fire a second time, but before he could pull the trigger, 'Doc' had shot him dead."

Of all the differing accounts of the incident, I personally prefer the latter. I mean, why should a fellow allow some drunken lout to go pouring hot lead into a crowded saloon? Why, one of those bullets might have hit one of the fellows who was losing to me at faro. *Then* where would I be?

So with one less obstruction to the local peace out of the way, I thought it time that I get in on the prosperity brought about by the Santa Fe's arrival to town. I found a partner by the name of Jordan J. Webb, who just happened to be the son of a very prosperous businessman and a friend of mine from Georgia; and on July 20, I contracted with carpenter W. G. Ward for the construction of a one-story clapboard saloon to be cobbled together on land that I had recently leased from Thomas L. Preston on the south side of Centre Street, a short block due west of the railroad station. The contract was for $372.50.

I also purchased an eight-foot strip of land adjoining the saloon in order to provide access to the gaming area at the rear of the bar.

I was delighted to learn that Hoodoo Brown had become the first acting magistrate in New Town. I was sure my worries about any legal ramifications from gambling would be mute.

Alas, such was not to be. Within a month of opening my new establishment, I was indicted for "keeping a gaming table," with bail set at $200. The next day I was indicted and charged with carrying a deadly weapon, with bail set at $100. Prosperity in New Mexico Territory, it seemed, was an elusive quarry.

Still, these were minor inconveniences to a man who had made a commitment to pursue the hot springs of Las Vegas and a cure for his consumptive disease. By building the Holliday Saloon and buying the adjoining land, just as by setting up my dental practice one more time, I had offered to myself and my woman a true commitment to the future. Kate liked Las Vegas. She liked being able to work in her own saloon without fear of being harassed or arrested—work that I never questioned so long as she continued to bring in money and share her welfare with me, as I did with her. As for myself, I enjoyed my employ, because I was able to keep more of the profits. Insofar as the arrests went, well, I just took that as part and parcel of the game.

So we settled into Las Vegas and were intent upon spending a good deal of our future there. Kate and I still had our little spats and quarrels from time to time, but by and large we were both finally happy.

At least we were until October 18, 1879. That's when everything changed. That's when Wyatt Earp arrived in town.

I was pleased as punch to see him, of course. It had been a long time since our paths had crossed. So when he told me about a new strike in Arizona and invited me to join the Earp brothers and their families in a new boomtown venture there, I had mixed feelings. I was always up for new adventures, and the thought of being taken into the Earp family fold like one of their own was appealing. But this venture, this time, I wasn't sure. This was different. I had not only my new business to consider, but also my commitment to Kate. How would she take uprooting ourselves yet one more time and following the sun ever west?

But Kate, being the loving, giving, sacrificing whore that she was, surprised me. After listening to Wyatt and me ramble on for several minutes, she thoughtfully agreed and—I think with a glint in her eye— said that we should sell the Holliday Saloon and leave Las Vegas as soon as possible for Tombstone. Kate wrote later, "[Wyatt] persuaded us to go to Arizona with them. We pulled out the next afternoon. There were seven of us in that outfit: Jim Earp, his wife and stepdaughter, Wyatt Earp, his wife, and Mr. and Mrs. John H. 'Doc' Holliday."

The Holliday and Earp party arrived in Prescott in November 1879, where we went to the home of Virgil and Allie Earp, who had been living there for the better part of two years. Mr. and Mrs. John H. Holliday had finally arrived in Arizona Territory.

A Town Called Tombstone

ORIENTAL SALOON INCIDENT

The Tombstone Nugget, *October 12, 1880*

Sunday night a disturbance in the Oriental Saloon between John Tyler and Doc Holliday, two well known sports, and a scene of bloodshed was imminent. Mutual friends, however, separated and disarmed them both, and Tyler went away, Holliday remaining in the saloon. M. E. Joyce, one of the proprietors, remonstrated with Holliday about creating a disturbance in the saloon and the conversation resulted with Holliday being bodily fired out by Joyce. The former came in and demanded his pistol from behind the bar, where it had been placed by the officer who disarmed him. It was not given him and he went out, but in a short time returned and walked toward Joyce, who was just coming from behind the bar, and with a remark that wouldn't look well in print, turned loose with a self-cocker. Joyce was not more than ten feet away and jumped for his assailant and struck him over the head with a six-shooter, felling him to the floor and lighting on top of him. Officers White and Bennett were near at hand and separated them, taking the pistol from each. Just how many shots were fired none present seem able to tell but in casting up accounts Joyce was found to be shot through the hand, his partner Mr. Parker, who was behind the bar, shot through the big toe of the left foot, and Holliday with a blow of the pistol in Joyce's hands. Gus Williams, barkeeper, was accused or [sic] firing a shot in the melee but in appearace [sic] in court yesterday morning no complaint appeared against him and the charge was dismissed. All parties directly implicated are still in bed and no direct arrests have been made, although a complaint has been entered against Holliday and he will be brought before Justice Reilly as soon as he is able to appear, probably to-day.

Kate and I left the Earps at Virgil's house that day and took a room at a local hotel. Wyatt, Virgil, and James sent word for their brother Morgan and his wife to join us in Prescott. I'm certain that Wyatt was looking forward to seeing them, since his brother and sister-in-law had been living for some time in Montana, quite a distance away. I wondered what Morg would think of this new wild and open country. I rather suspected he would enjoy it.

Of course, our ultimate goal was to travel on to Tombstone, but for the time being, Prescott would do just fine. It was an amiable enough place to hang one's hat. Founded in 1863 following a gold strike, it was in that respect little different from most western communities. Back in those days most towns were founded as a result of a silver or gold strike—some panner discovering a few nuggets in a creek bed or a wash or occasionally buried a shallow way beneath the ground. Either that or the military came out and constructed a fort to protect the settlers on their endless journey west, and a group of enterprising business folks followed on their heels and slapped a few buildings together and hung out a few signs and, the next thing you knew, you had yourself a town.

Situated on the banks of the Granite Creek, Prescott served as the capital of the new Territory of Arizona, which had been carved off from the New Mexico Territory by an act of Congress in 1863. The town's main industry had mostly forever been mining and timber.

It didn't take much time at all for me to find a faro game, and before long my winnings were substantial. I saw in Prescott a town that was ripe for the taking; and by God, I meant to lend a hand personally toward that goal. After about a week, though, the Earps were ready to depart Prescott for Tombstone, but I decided to stay behind, in an effort to continue reaping the benefits of the sporting crowd. A gambling man is nothing if not a gambler.

So Kate and I bid the Earps ado, and we remained behind to see things through to their natural conclusion. But on March 2, 1880, things took a turn for the worse as the village of Prescott passed an ordinance requiring a monthly assessment on each gaming table in town. Think about that. The town also passed another ordinance requiring a fine of not less than $10 nor more than $300 for discharging a firearm within the corporate limits. Even more legislative restrictions were rumored to follow.

Thus it had become imminently clear to me and my beloved that the opportune moment to depart Prescott had arrived sooner than later. Kate and I headed back to New Mexico so that I could conclude some unfinished business there, not the least of which was appearing on March 12, 1880, at the San Manuel County District Courthouse to face charges of keeping a gaming table and carrying a deadly weapon. The more some things change . . .

Of course, the charges being more an opportunity for the town to manufacture some income than a means of controlling crime in the streets, they were dismissed at the request of the district attorney. He was, after all, a practical man. I, in turn, recovered my costs, which included the $300 bail I had previously posted for the two cases. I paid my fines and—with the money left over—paid the carpenter I had hired to build the Holliday Saloon on Centre Street. With the outstanding lien against the property finally paid, I was free and clear of debt once more. I was an honest man.

I stopped by the local saloon on the Plaza in Old Town where I ran into Charlie White, who was employed there as a bartender. Two years earlier, in 1878, we'd had a ruckus in Dodge, when I accused White of theft and chased him out of town. He obviously neither forgot nor forgave, for as soon as he spotted me, he drew his pistol and started firing. I dove for cover, pulled my own gun from inside my coat, and returned the favor. White grabbed for his head and fell hard to the floor. Even though it was a clear case of self-defense, I decided the wisest course of action was to depart for New Town and the protection that the unincorporated part of the city provided its honest citizenry there.

Fortunately for me, and even more so for White, it turned out that the bullet had only grazed him. Stunned, he'd fallen to the floor. Once he had regained consciousness, he grabbed the first train out of town for Boston, apparently no longer content in pressing his luck by going up against the notorious Doc Holliday.

Now that was a curious train of events—the emergence of a mild-mannered tubercular dentist from honest law-abiding citizen to someone of great notoriety and even greater alleged prowess with a gun. I say alleged because, if truth be known, I had not been in that many scrapes involving the use of a weapon. True, I had carved one blackguard into pieces during a card game, but that was solely in self-defense. I had come to Wyatt Earp's aid on another occasion—again, not unjustifiably so. Yet, my reputation as a leather-slinging pistoleer of some prowess had given rise not only to tall tales that made me snicker when first I heard them, but also to horrifying accounts of a coldhearted killer with mayhem on his mind.

I owed part of that, I suppose, to my growing friendship with Wyatt. For as his reputation was already solidly hewn for some time, so too did it seem natural that I would be of similar background and temperament. I owed part, too, I am certain, to my sweet dove Kate, who enjoyed regaling her friends—males, mostly—of the lightning-fast prowess with a drawn pistol that her own man, John Henry "Doc" Holliday, possessed. In doing so, she naturally took some perverted sort of pride. Kate was nothing if not filled with a love for the blarney that has made the Irish so famed. I am surprised she had none of the Isle of Man in her background. Or none of which I knew.

Kate also liked telling tall tales of the savage beast to whom she was betrothed (or married, it depended upon the circumstances and the group of people to whom she was testifying) to prevent her johnnies from becoming too possessive or disposed toward violence. Her occupation was not without its inherent hazards, of course. How comforting it must have been to know that the man she was entertaining at the time was fully aware that her own beloved killer of men was not too far distant.

In any event, I took in all of the tall tales with a fair amount of amusement, and not a little pride, if I might say. I *was* a fast draw, no doubt about it, faster perhaps than even the great Wyatt Earp. But Wyatt, my good friend, was a much more accurate shot than I and could do damage to a man that would render him *nolo contendere* for all eternity, whereas I—regardless of my speed on the draw—was fortunate to hit the side of a barn.

Unfortunately for me, that fact rarely slowed me in reacting to any injustice thrown my way, whether real or imagined. I must admit that my growing consumption of alcoholic beverages fueled my fury—and dulled my aim, if truth be known. It is more difficult to strike at thirty paces a moving target when your vision is blurred from grain alcohol than when not. I suppose, if intellect prevailed, I would have recognized that fact and lessened my consumption of the stuff of which dreams are made had it not also tended to dull the nearly constant chest pain in which I increasingly found myself. I could have relied more on medications such as morphine or laudanum and less on Kentucky sipping whiskey. But that would have led to an entirely new set of problems; as a medical practitioner, I chose rather to avoid that option for as long as I possibly could.

So, after settling my scores in Las Vegas, I returned to Prescott, where I met some old friends who invited me to stay with them in their home. Since Kate had decided not to make the trip with me—following yet another one of our many and ever-escalating spats—I took them up on their offer. Not long thereafter, Wyatt sent me a letter saying that

William Bat Masterson (1853–1921) was a lawman
and friend to Doc and the Earps throughout his
career. KANSAS STATE HISTORICAL SOCIETY

This photograph of John H. Holliday was taken upon the occasion of his graduation from dental college and is the only known historically accurate photo of him as a young man. The photo was most likely taken in 1882, when Holliday was 21 years of age. INTERNATIONAL FEATURES SYNDICATE

This photograph appears to be a heavily retouched original—or possibly even an artist's rendering—of a subject who may or may not actually have been John H. Holliday, although many historians think it is most likely a rendering of Doc in his early thirties. It may have been taken when he was in Tombstone, Arizona. It is important to remember that newspapermen thought little of altering photos during the late nineteenth and early twentieth centuries. Photos of Doc were sometimes altered or retouched to make him appear more sinister, in keeping with his rapidly growing reputation. KANSAS STATE HISTORICAL SOCIETY

Another photograph that appears to be of J. H. Holliday was purportedly taken shortly before Doc went to Tombstone to join his friends, the Earps, prior to the shootout at the O.K. Corral. The handwriting reads "Yours Truly, J. H. Holliday." INTERNATIONAL FEATURES SYNDICATE

A photograph of Dodge House, where Doc Holliday roomed and kept his dental practice. Doc ran a notice in the *Dodge City Times* on June 8, 1878, announcing his arrival: "John H. Holliday, Dentist, very respectfully offers his professional services to the citizens of Dodge City and surrounding county during the summer. Office at Room No. 24 Dodge House. Where satisfaction is not given, money will be refunded."
KANSAS STATE HISTORICAL SOCIETY

Headstone of John H. "Doc" Holliday, Linwood Cemetery, Glenwood Springs, Colorado. The first published report of his death, which appeared in the *Aspen Daily Times*, said simply and eloquently: "Glenwood Springs, Colo., November 8.—Doc Holliday died here this morning at the Hotel Glenwood and was buried this afternoon and was followed to the cemetery by a large number of kindred spirits." INTERNATIONAL FEATURES SYNDICATE

Dodge City Peace Commission, 1883, one of the most famous photographs in pioneer history. Standing (left to right) are William H. Harris, Luke Short, William Bat Masterson, W. F. Petillon. Seated (left to right) are Charles E. Bassett, Wyatt Earp, Frank McLain, Neil Brown. KANSAS STATE HISTORICAL SOCIETY

Wyatt Earp (1848–1929), circa 1887, was a steadfast friend of Doc and a lawman in several western towns. This photo was taken while he was running saloons and dabbling in real estate in San Diego, following Doc's death in Glenwood Springs, Colorado. INTERNATIONAL FEATURES SYNDICATE

Tombstone was a very lively and prosperous town where I could do well. He mentioned in an aside that there was no dentist there.

I telegraphed Kate and told her of my plans and that I would join her to begin the next leg of our journey together shortly. I detected in her reply that she was less than enthusiastic with the prospect. "If you are going to tie yourself to the Earp Brothers, go to it," she wrote. "I am going to Globe." I wrote her back that it was fine with me and that I'd meet her in Globe as soon as I could, and we would decide from there where our tumultuous relationship would lead us.

When I finally met up with her again in Las Vegas, I told her that I didn't think I would care all that much for Tombstone. From what I had read and what I had heard, it was too common, too plebian a village for me. So the two of us set off together, and when we got as far as Gillette, we stopped over but had difficulty finding a room, since there were none available. As fortune would have it, a complete stranger who we had met purely by chance, a Mr. Webber, told us we could sleep on the bed in his office. The next morning Kate and I started out again, she to Globe and I, temporarily at least, to Tombstone.

I arrived in that town in September 1880 to find the Earp Brothers well entrenched within the community. Virgil was a deputy United States marshal, a position he had taken while still in Prescott. Before departing for Tombstone in January 1881, Wyatt had taken a job as a shotgun messenger for the Wells, Fargo Company. In July of that same year, he had been appointed deputy sheriff of Pima County. James was working as a bartender in a bowling alley on Allen Street across from the Crystal Palace Saloon.

Shortly after arriving in twon, the Earps had begun acquiring various mining claims and real estate. Morgan and his wife, Lou, had arrived from Montana in the spring of 1880. Before leaving Montana, he had been a policeman in Butte. After arriving in Arizona he quickly involved himself in his brothers' business investments as well as in the various activities of the saloons and gaming parlors.

With my good friends so deeply rooted in the economic aspects of the town, I wasted little time in joining them in their various business pursuits. Wyatt and I jointly purchased some water rights and a little real estate, while we continued to supplement our income with our winnings at poker and faro.

Before long, I had become a regular visitor at the swank Oriental Saloon at the corner of Allen and Fifth streets. It had opened two months before I had come to town. The *Tombstone Epitaph* hailed it as the most "elegantly furnished saloon this side of the favored city of the Golden Gate." Inside, a carved bar finished in white and gilt reposed off to the right of the main entranceway, setting off a second clubroom in the rear, where the sporting element plied their trade. The owners of the Oriental knew their business, and soon everyone who was anyone looking for a game looked there first.

But a group of disgruntled gamblers hoped to encourage a small-time criminal by the name of Johnny Tyler to cause trouble in the Oriental in an attempt to dissuade customers from playing there. The three owners of the saloon sold Wyatt a one-quarter interest in the gambling concession in August 1880 as insurance against anyone causing any further nonsense. They knew full well that Wyatt would be backed to the teeth by his brothers and friends, including the notorious Doc Holliday, in the event that any trouble should erupt.

It had been a fortuitous venture on the owners' behalf, for, sure enough, on October 11, 1880, Johnny Tyler entered the saloon and, feeling his whiskey, began making a stir.

Now, Tyler was no friend of mine. A braggart and a cocky little man of no conceivable value to anyone, he was a card shark and a cheat, and whenever he entered a game, all elements of chance flew out the window.

Of course, he assumed that I was equally scurrilous. When he accused me of double-dealing, I picked up a glass of whiskey, sipped from it lightly, and threw the remainder into his face—an act that pained me to the quick, I confess—at which occurrence he leaped upon me, knocking me backwards off my chair. The two of us rolled around, thrashing about the floor for several minutes like two randy roosters, before a group of locals pulled us apart and took our pistols and handed them to the barkeep to hold in order to prevent further trouble.

At that, Tyler left the saloon. I brushed myself off and righted my chair, and I sat down to continue the game.

Within moments one of the Oriental's proprietors, Milton Joyce, who was never too fond of me for my closeness to the Earps, approached, saying to the effect that my kind was no longer welcome in his establishment. I replied that, to the best of my knowledge, my kind was no more objectionable upon the premises than his kind, and since he was welcome there, so too would I remain.

Joyce ordered me out once again, to which warning I would have been perfectly happy to oblige, except that he still had in his possession my favorite pistol from the earlier ruckus, and I was not about to leave without it.

You see, when a man loses his woman to another man, it is a serious matter. When a man loses his horse to another man, it is unforgivable. But when a man loses his gun to another man, it is inconceivable. Still, not wanting to escalate the fray, I gave Joyce my word as a gentleman to take my revolver in hand and leave peaceably.

"Your word!" Joyce yelled. "Get your fucking ass out of here before I kick it out into the street again, and if you come back one more time, I'll lay you out where you stand."

That being more than what a true southern gentleman should ever be asked to endure, I repeated my demand for my gun, saying that I would leave only after he turned it over to me, whereupon he leaped out from behind the bar, grabbed me by my collar, and threw me out into the street, warning me not to come back.

I picked myself up and walked purposefully down the block to my room and returned to the saloon several minutes later, armed with a double-action revolver. When Joyce saw me with my hand on my pistol, he grabbed a revolver of his own and coldcocked me with the butt of the gun, knocking me to the floor. As I tried to rise, he leaped upon me, and in the ensuing scuffle, several shots were fired. I somehow managed even in my stupored state to shoot Joyce in the hand and one of his partners, William C. Parker, in the left foot. I was apparently hooking my shots. I was summarily hauled off to jail, booked, and released.

The following morning, feeling strangely refreshed and invigorated despite the previous evening's repartee, I finished my breakfast and walked the half block to the courthouse, where Judge Reilly noted that none of my accusers had shown up for the hearing, at which point he fined me $20, returned my pistol, and told me I was free to leave.

I asked the judge what damage I had managed to inflict upon the miscreants the night before, and he replied that I had shot Joyce through the hand and his partner in the big toe.

"That is very vexing news indeed," I said.

"I should think it would be," the judge replied.

"Yes," I said. "I'm a *much* better shot than *that*."

Thief in the Night

I had learned that Joyce was out of commission for the next couple of weeks. The gunshot wound I had inflicted to his hand was so severe that doctors feared its complete loss. Naturally, during this time, Joyce's feelings of contempt and hatred toward me continued to mount, as they did toward the entire Earp clan. He was not happy that Wyatt owned a share in the Oriental. That made for bad blood.

Several days later I met an old friend, William Leonard, a jeweler who had occupied a storefront in the same building as my dental office on Bridge Street in Las Vegas. I had always liked Leonard, and he, me. I don't know why. Nevertheless, it was a friendship that was destined to cause me a great deal of trouble later in life. But for the nonce, our relationship was widely acknowledged. Wyatt wrote of it, "Holiday [*sic*] was a friend of Leonard's, having known him in Las Vegas New Mexico where Leonard was established in the jewelry business. And was considered at the time, a respectable citizen. And from Las Vegas, he came to Tombstone and with Harry Head, Jim Crane and Bill King and himself all went batching in a house two miles north from town, which was known as the Wells. And all three remained there for several months. Holiday [*sic*] would make them a visit now and then knowing Leonard so well, which many people knew how friendly they were. Doc and Leonard had resumed their friendship in Tombstone."

On Tuesday, March 15, 1881, I rode out of town to visit Billy King at the Wells. The light snow that had fallen overnight was just enough "to whiten everything and it looked very pretty."

Wyatt fairly accurately summed things up later, saying, "Holiday [*sic*] went to the livery stable on this day, hired a saddle horse which he did quite often to visit Leonard at the Wells. The horse came from Dunbar's stable. . . . Holiday [*sic*] remained there until 4 P.M. Old man Fuller was hauling water into Tombstone at that time, and leaving the Wells with a load of water Holiday [*sic*] tied his Horse behind the wagon and rode into town with Fuller and which many people knew. After Holliday ate his dinner, he went to playing faro. And he was still playing when the word came to Tombstone from Bob Paul to me that there had been a holdup."

After finishing dinner, as Wyatt said, I did join several other regulars for a long night of cards at the Alhambra Saloon. I was feeling my usual self—that is to say, not very good. I had been coughing quite a bit that night, bringing up phlegm and a fair amount of pus—never a good sign—which I tried to hide as much as I could in a white silk handkerchief. The coughing had been going on for several weeks virtually nonstop, preventing me from devoting as much time to my dental practice as I should have. I know that might sound old by now, for it seems as if I have said that on numerous occasions. But you have to understand that, when you are a medical practitioner in charge of the health and welfare of a patient and you are unable to concentrate on matters at hand—matters that could very well affect the future health and well-being of someone who has placed his or her trust in you—all desire to pursue your chosen profession falls by the wayside. With my income from dentistry severely curtailed, it was understandable that I would turn my attentions more to matters of the evening. That, in turn, merely exacerbated my problems, causing my consumption to worsen and my intrinsically genial personality to fade.

Not only that, but I was soon to learn that my troubles in Tombstone had only begun. Earlier that evening, before the game started, J. D. Kinnear's Arizona Mail and Stage Company's coach had left Tombstone for Benson, Arizona. It was hauling with it nine passengers and approximately $80,000 in silver bullion. Now, I'm telling you, this was a full stage. Eight people inside and one in the dickey seat on the back, *plus* all that silver. Coaches don't get much more loaded than that.

And word must have gotten out, because at around ten o'clock, as the stage neared Drew's Station about a mile north of Contention City, a group of outlaws swarmed down on it. Eli Bud Philpott, the regular driver, had felt ill that evening and handed the reins off to Bob Paul, who normally rode shotgun. Philpott, in turn, took over Paul's job. As the robbers opened fire, they killed both Philpott and the passenger who was riding in the dickey on top of the coach. Paul managed to return fire, eventually turning back the robbers. At the sound of the gunfire, the horses had bolted, and it took Paul several attempts to rein them back in.

When he finally pulled the stage into Benson, Paul sent a telegram to Wells, Fargo agent Marshall Williams in Tombstone, telling him about the thwarted robbery. Williams quickly assembled a posse that included the three Earp brothers and Bat Masterson, who had recently come to town and was dealing at the Oriental. Bob Paul joined them, and the posse lit out of town for the holdup scene.

A few minutes later County Sheriff John Behan called upon Frank Leslie and William Breackenridge to form a second posse, and they rode off into the night hell-bent for leather. The Earp posse had located a trail leading from the site of the holdup to the Dragoon Mountains at Helms Ranch, where it turned north to Tres Alamos. Three days later, after a hard ride that led up the San Pedro River, they came upon Len Redfield's ranch, where Behan's group joined them. After a brief questioning Morgan Earp arrested Luther King, who had confessed to holding the horses during the attempted robbery. Facing the gallows himself, King quickly gave up the names of his accomplices, including Harry the Kid Head, Jim Crane, and my old friend William Leonard.

The next morning the *Tombstone Epitaph* ran an article saying that there had been eight holdup men, a fact that was subsequently corroborated by the passengers on the stage. Behan insisted on taking custody of the prisoner back to Tombstone while the Earp party continued on the trail of the other three suspects that King had named. Back in town the next morning, rumors rapidly circulated that the four other robbery suspects were likely Ike Clanton, Curly Bill Brocius, Pete Spencer, and Frank Stilwell. Not surprisingly, because of my friendship with William Billy Leonard, rumors circulated that I had been implicated in the robbery attempt as well.

I mean, can you believe it? I am sitting at a friendly game of poker back in town when the robbery occurs, and I am being touted as one of the toughs! I tell you, I was beginning to feel that taking the high road through life will only lead you to a better view of perdition. Worse, the only way I could see my name clear was to help catch those responsible so that the whole truth could be revealed.

But it was not to be. Luther King had been placed under custody of undersheriff Harry Woods. Woods, an addle-minded fellow with an intense loyalty to Behan, allowed King to escape by walking out of the unlocked back door to the jail. Woods, who was also editor of the *Tombstone Nugget,* published a self-defensive account of the escape shortly after.

[King] escaped from the Sheriff's office by quietly stepping out the back door while Harry Jones, Esq., was drawing up a bill of sale for a horse the prisoner was selling to John Dunbar. Undersheriff Harry Woods and Dunbar were present. He *[King]* had been absent but a few seconds before he was missed. A confederate on the outside had a horse in readiness for him. It was a well-planned job by outsiders to get him away. He was an important witness against Holliday.

Of course, there was no confederate outside the jail. There didn't *have* to be. It was a setup from day one, and it had Behan's brand all over it! Luckily, some residents saw the escape for what it actually was. One, a fellow by the name of George Parsons, kept a diary throughout those years of lawlessness in Tombstone and wrote, "King the stage robber escaped tonight early from H. Woods, who had been previously notified of an attempt at release to be made. Some of our officials should be hanged. They're a bad lot."

Things turned yet worse for me when, on March 24, the *Arizona Weekly Star* published a report substantiating Woods' biased account. The Tucson paper reported that three of the robbers, Head, Crane, and Leonard, were headed for Mexico by way of Tucson. "The fourth [alleged to be Doc] is at Tombstone and is well known and has been shadowed ever since his return." Everybody, it seems, had completely forgotten about Luther King and his admission to being involved in the foiled holdup. Nobody wanted to believe Doc Holliday was innocent!

Although there was no evidence supporting my involvement in any way, the Cowboys quickly jumped at the chance to tie me to the stage killings. My problems only worsened when Behan and his bunch let it be known that they suspected me of being the eighth participant. Apparently, it was their way of camouflaging their own association with the very criminal elements who had committed the murders, as well as numerous other crimes, while shifting the blame to me. Behan was a close friend of Milt Joyce, who shared no love for me—*or* for the Earps. Additionally, Behan's relationship with Wyatt was shaky to say the least. Behan had reneged on an agreement he had made in order to get Wyatt to pull out of the race for sheriff so that he could win. Ever since, he and Wyatt had been scrapping. Looking at Wyatt as his greatest political rival, Behan would have loved nothing more than to tie Wyatt's good friend, Doc Holliday, to the murders. Behan was also jealous of the looks his stunning girlfriend, Josie, had been casting Wyatt's way of late. I only wished she had cast them upon yours truly.

In any event, less than one month after the double killings, I found myself in trouble with the law once more when I was indicted in the court of Judge Elbert O. Wallace in the case, the *Territory of Arizona v. J. H. Holliday*. The indictment charged me with "threats against life" and "attempting to kill a saloon keeper, who objected to his presence in the house." The truth is that, when that mongrel Joyce called me a stage robber, I took offense, and I cuffed him with my hand alongside his head. A number of people jumped in to separate us before the fight could escalate, much the pity, and I may have made some reference to the value of his life throughout his limited days left on earth. But nothing anyone would have taken seriously. Not really.

Still, I was relieved when the charges against me were dismissed upon my agreement to pay all court costs.

But more black clouds railed over me when Behan and Joyce got together with some of the Cowboys to lay the groundwork for yet another legal charge. On May 27, 1881, I was indicted for a felony in the federal court of District Justice W. H. Stilwell. The charge involved the Kinnear stage robbery attempt and two murders. Because the stage had been carrying mail for the U.S. government, its attempted holdup was a federal offense. Although not formally charged, I was called to court to be questioned and investigated. I appeared dutifully with my attorney, A. G. D. George, on June 2, 3, 4, and 6, each appearance ending in a continuance. Finally, the case was continued to the next session and yet another continuance before being stricken from the calendar.

My next run-in with the legal system occurred as a result of an unlikely alliance. Kate had come to town from Globe to help celebrate the Fourth of July with me. It didn't take long before the two of us began scrapping, and Kate went out on the town for a night of drinking with Johnny Behan and Milt Joyce. I spent the time playing cards. Little did I realize that Kate, stupid sweet drunken whore that she was, began telling tales about me until Behan finally persuaded her to sign an affidavit stating that I had admitted to committing the two stage murders to her. The following morning, armed with the affidavit, Behan arrested me for murder. Bail was set at $5,000 in the *Territory of Arizona* v. *John H. Holliday*. I might never have gotten out of jail on that one if it hadn't been for the extraordinary efforts of Wyatt Earp, along with the backing of a couple of local sureties who put up my bond.

Of course Kate had by then sobered up, paid her fine for being drunk and disorderly, and immediately regretted what she had done. She and Wyatt went to court where she repudiated her statement under oath before Judge Wells Spicer, who dismissed the charges of murder against me on July 9, saying there was no evidence whatsoever to show the guilt of the defendant.

One more time, Behan had failed to implicate me. And one more time, Kate, filled with shame, left town for Globe. To tell you the truth, I was glad to see her go.

And sad.

It was the middle of July, and I realized that I had spent most of that summer either denying on the streets or fighting in the courts the trumped-up charges that had been leveled against me. All the while, the real killers continued on their tear throughout the territory.

On June 10 Bill Leonard and Harry the Kid Head stopped by a store in Eureka in New Mexico Territory. After an afternoon of heavy drinking, they confided to the shopkeeper their very ominous intent: they had set out to kill Ike and Bill Haslett in order to take over the prosperous Haslett Ranch in the Animas Valley. The Haslett Ranch was sandwiched between two other spreads, both owned by Mike Gray, a former Tombstone justice of the peace, who had taken a wrong turn somewhere on the road to hell and aligned himself with the Cowboys, one of whom was his own son, Dick. With Dixie Gray controlling the three ranches, the Cowboys would find their hideout nearly impregnable. What a perfect place to hole themselves up, not to mention their stolen cattle. As fortune would have it, a friend of the Hasletts overheard the plot and warned the two brothers of the plan of attack. By the time Bill Leonard and Harry Head had sobered up and ridden out to the ranch, the Hasletts had hidden themselves behind the corral and ambushed and killed the two gunmen. Leonard, they learned, still wore the battle scars he had received during the Kinnear stage holdup.

On Saturday, June 18, the *Tombstone Epitaph* ran an article about the killings of Leonard and Head. That meant that the only other known member of the Kinnear stage holdup gang who could clear my name was Jim Crane.

Upon learning that Leonard and Head had been killed, Crane organized a party of Cowboys to avenge their deaths. On June 12 they rode into Eureka just as the Haslett brothers were riding out. After a twenty-five-mile chase, they caught up with the two men and opened fire. The Hasletts, to their credit, killed two of the Cowboys and wounded a third before succumbing to a rainfall of flying lead. Both Ike and Bill lay dead in their tracks.

I knew I didn't have much time to catch up with Crane before he, too, became a victim. Worse still, he had by now already gotten word that we were on his trail. The lawlessness and killings in the area had reached such extreme proportions that the United States War Department had issued an all-out warning. U.S. Attorney General Isaac W. MacVeigh expressed concern about the ongoing lawlessness, robberies, and cattle rustling on both sides of the Mexican border and called upon federal, state, county, and local law enforcement agencies, as well as the Mexican Federales, to join the fight in securing the peace. MacVeigh went so far as to send a deputy and a posse after the Cowboys at an estimated cost of $5,000 to $10,000. In addition to that bounty, Wells, Fargo offered a reward of $1,200 each for the capture of Leonard, Head, and Crane. Wyatt, ever watchful and always one step ahead, came up with an idea that should have worked like a charm.

After secretly meeting with Ike Clanton, Frank McLaury, and Joe Hill, Wyatt offered to turn over all the money from the rewards to them if they would reveal where the stage killers were holed up. No doubt he was anxious to reap the glory from catching Crane in order to enhance his own political prospects in the upcoming election for sheriff of Cochise County, but he had another motive, I'm sure. He wanted to nab Crane in order to clear my name of any implications in the killings.

Of course, Leonard and Head were already dead. When Ike Clanton and Joe Hill informed Wyatt that Crane had been seen at old Man Clanton's ranch near Cloverdale, New Mexico Territory, Wyatt, who had been deputized by his brother Virgil, formed a posse that included brothers Morgan and Warren and me to pursue Crane and whatever other Cowboys were with him.

We saddled up that morning and lit out of Tombstone, slapping leather for the area where the Arizona and New Mexico territories met Mexico's states of Sonora and Chihuahua. Morgan picked up a trail and, on a hunch, we followed it to an area called Devil's Kitchen in Skeleton Canyon. There we found a herd of cattle and a group of drovers working them north. They consisted of some of the mangiest lawbreakers this side of Hades—Old Man Clanton, Dixie Gray, Charles Bud Snow, William Lang, Billy Byers, Harry Ernshaw, and none other than Jim Crane. They were in the process of driving the herd of rustled Mexican cattle to Tombstone for market.

Just before the sun broke over the canyon walls the following morning, we called to them to surrender, and when they went for their guns, we opened fire, riddling the camp with lead. The Cowboys, determined not to be taken prisoners, returned our fire, which was a fatal mistake. The entire incident was over in a matter of moments. We knew only Harry Ernshaw to have escaped, although we later learned that Billy Byers, who had been shot in the gut and the arm and feigned death to escape capture, also eventually managed to get away. Among those who weren't so lucky: Jim Crane, the last of the stage murderers that Luther King had fingered. The last man alive who could have cleared my name in the robbery attempt and killings.

We had hoped to take Crane prisoner, of course, but life does not always go the way we hope. To make matters worse, I had been wounded in the leg during the skirmish, as had Warren. Wyatt, with his usual nod to Dame Fortune, escaped without a scratch.

After returning to Tombstone, Warren decided to leave for his parents' home in California to recuperate. When he came back to Arizona, he was still limping, as was I. I had spent my thirtieth birthday, August 14, 1881, learning to walk with a cane.

It was no fun.

Several weeks after the gunfight, Kate left Globe to return to Tombstone, where we reunited. Despite all of our squabbles, she was really a loving and caring wench for whom the site of my injury brought out the best in her as she set about personally overseeing my restoration.

By October I was walking much better and intent upon repaying Kate in kindness for her months of doting care. I invited her to the San Agustin fiesta in Tucson for a week of music, dancing, food, drink, and, of course, faro.

I confess I had an ulterior motive for going. The federal court there was scheduled to hear the case of Pete "Spence" Spencer and Frank Stilwell, the two accused of robbing the Sandy Bob stage on its way from Tombstone to Bisbee on September 8, 1881. They had supposedly netted some $2,500 from the Wells, Fargo strongbox and another $600 from the passengers. A Bisbee boot maker identified the distinctive prints of Stilwell's boots as the same ones found at the scene of the robbery.

The two brigands each were eventually released on a $2,000 bond, just as they were rearrested by Deputy U.S. Marshal Virgil Earp, this time on federal warrants for robbing the U.S. mail. Behan wasn't the only man in town who knew how to use the law to his own advantage.

The new hearing was scheduled for October 20 in Tucson. The Earps anticipated the Cowboys showing up to post bail for the two, and we all wanted to be there to make sure that didn't happen.

After Kate and I had spent four days at the fiesta, I found myself in a local cantina bucking at faro when Kate came up behind me and placed her open hand on my left shoulder. Not far behind, Morgan came up and leaned down to whisper in my ear.

"Doc, we want you in Tombstone tomorrow. Better come up this evening." "What's up?"

"Bad business," he said.

I hesitated before showing him my hand.

His eyes widened, he paused, and then he motioned with his head toward the door.

I played out my hand, drew in my winnings, and told him, "Let's go."

I cashed in my chips and Morg told me to have Kate stay behind.

I turned to her and said, "You'd better stay here. I'll come after you tomorrow, or in a day or two."

Kate turned to me and said, "No, I am going with you."

Morg told her that we would have to take a freight train. She said, "If you can go on a freight, so can I."

I told her, "We're going to Benson on a freight, then we have to ride in an open buckboard. It's not going to be an easy trip."

She said, "If you can ride in an open buckboard, so can I."

I turned to Morgan. He squinted back at me. "Well, what do you say, Doc?"

There was a sense of hopelessness in his voice. There was a sense of possession in hers. For some reason, neither one bothered me that night.

"Well," I said, glancing from one to the other. "It looks like we're going to Tombstone."

Shootout at the O.K. Corral

Kate and I checked into Fly's boarding house around ten o'clock on the evening of October 25, 1881. I kissed her on the cheek and told her to go up to our room and I would join her later. Then Morg and I left for the Alhambra Saloon.

On the very same Tuesday evening upon which we entered Tombstone, Ike Clanton had already returned to town. He had left Tucson for his ranch near Charleston. From there, he proceeded to Sulphur Spring Valley, where he holed up for three days before moving on to town.

Ike had become increasingly vexed with the Earps and me, believing that Wyatt had disclosed their secret agreement to turn over the reward money to Clanton in exchange for revealing the location of the Kinnear stagecoach murderers. Wyatt had shown Clanton a telegram from Marsh Williams that outlined the details of the Wells, Fargo reward terms. Ike's natural sense of paranoia led him to assume that Williams had shared the information with Wyatt because Wyatt had told him of his secret plan. Knowing that Wyatt was my best friend, he assumed as well that Wyatt had made me privy to their agreement. In so believing, Ike knew that set him in a bad place. If any of the other Cowboys found out about the deal, Ike would be in for trouble. He did not like the thought that Wyatt and I held the power of life and death over him.

That evening, Clanton hunted down Wyatt and whined in his high-pitched voice that the lawman had revealed their secret. When Wyatt denied the fact, Ike shouted that Doc Holliday had told him that even *he* knew of the pact. Wyatt once again denied the allegation and said that he would prove it as soon as I returned to Tombstone from Tucson.

Later, at the Alhambra, Wyatt cornered me at the bar and shared his earlier discussion with Clanton, saying that Ike had accused him of revealing the details of the secret business arrangement between the two of them. I told Wyatt that I hadn't a clue as to what he was referring and added that nothing in particular coming from the lips of a lying snake such as Ike Clanton could ever be of interest to me. Apparently satisfied, Wyatt turned and walked away.

After several hours of card playing, hunger got the better of me, and I went to A. D. Walsh's Can Can Lunch and Eating Counter, located in the front of the Alhambra, opposite the bar. There I ran into none other than Ike Clanton himself.

"Ike, you're a son of a bitch of a Cowboy," I cursed. Clanton, trying to cover his tracks, told me that he had revealed to Wyatt the location of Jim Crane and the others only in a last-ditch attempt to lure the Earps and me out of town so that the Cowboys could kill us. I took him at his word and snapped, "You son of a bitch, if you ain't healed, go and heal yourself!" I told him that I had been in the group that had killed his cattle-rustling father, and I was looking forward to being in the group that would someday kill him.

Virgil Earp, who was Tombstone's city marshal, came up and threatened to arrest us both if we didn't stop quarreling. We glared hard at one another before parting, after which Wyatt and I left the Alhambra and walked up Allen Street. After a short time we stopped, and Wyatt held out his hand.

"What's this for?" I asked.

He smiled. "I just wanted to let you know how much I appreciate all the backing-up you've given me over the years."

Taken momentarily aback—and I assure you, that is very unfamiliar territory—I took his hand and shook it before I watched him turn up the street to return home to Mattie. I went to find Kate at Fly's Boarding House.

In the meantime Ike had gone down to the Occidental Saloon, where he drank and played poker until after sunup. Others at the table included Tom McLaury, Cochise County sheriff Johnny Behan, and Virgil Earp, who sat in the game in an attempt to diffuse any problems that might arise. As daylight broke over the horizon, Virg got up and left the game, saying that he was going to bed. Clanton told them he wanted him to take a message to me. When Virg asked what the message was, Ike said, "The damned son of a bitch has got to fight." Virg told him he would deliver no such message, saying that he was an officer of the law and didn't want any trouble.

"You won't carry the message? You may have to fight before you know it!"

Clanton cashed in his chips and left the saloon when he ran into Ned Boyle on the walk in front of the telegraph office. Boyle was a bartender from Kelly's Wine Room. Clanton told Boyle and anyone else he later encountered that I had insulted him the night before and that he wanted to fight. Clanton then went on to Kelly's, which served as both a saloon and a retail liquor shop, for one more round. It lasted until after 11 a.m., after which Clanton stopped at the Capitol Saloon before staggering down Fourth Street, bragging about his intention to kill the Earps and me. A policeman who overheard what he'd said went straight to Virgil's house and awakened him. At the same time, Ned Boyle went to inform Wyatt of Clanton's threats. "There's serious trouble brewing."

Virgil dressed quickly and left his house and found Clanton between Fremont and Allen streets, walking down Fourth with a Winchester rifle in one hand and a pistol stuck inside his pants. Wyatt emerged at just the same time, and Clanton started shouting at both brothers before Virgil pulled out his gun and buffaloed him alongside the ear. Virgil arrested him for carrying firearms, which was a violation of Tombstone City Ordinance Number 9. Virgil and Wyatt hauled the bleeding Cowboy before Judge Albert Wallace's court, where Wallace found him guilty and fined him $25 on a concealed-weapons charge. Virgil left to take Clanton's weapons over to the Grand Hotel for safekeeping. Wyatt wasn't quite done yet.

"You damned dirty cow thief," he told the Cowboy. "You have been threatening our lives, and I know it. I think I would be justified in shooting you down any place I should meet you, but if you are anxious for a fight, I will go anywhere on earth to make a fight with you, even over to San Simon among your crowd." As Wyatt departed the courtroom, he ran into Tom McLaury, also struggling to throw off the nightlong card game and drink fest. By that time word had gotten out and traveled throughout the entire Cowboy camp about the rapidly mounting tensions between the Earps and their group, and when McLaury confronted Wyatt, a scuffle broke out. Wyatt pulled his gun and coldcocked him across the left side of his head, dropping him to the ground before walking away, muttering, "I could kill the son of a bitch."

After paying his fine and having a doctor tend to his head wound, Clanton went out to find me. He had retrieved his guns from the hotel and come down to Fly's Boarding House around 1:30 in the afternoon. I was still in bed sound asleep. When Mrs. Fly intercepted Clanton in the lobby, she told him she didn't know if I was in or not. Clanton took a quick look around and left.

Molly Fly told Kate that Ike was searching for me. When Kate brought me news that Clanton was looking for me, I told her, "If God will let me live to get my clothes on, he shall see me."

I pulled on one of my favorite pastel shirts, a pair of fresh undershorts, and a dark gray suit, all meticulously cleaned and pressed. I placed my hat on my head and, because of the cold weather, threw on a long gray Ulster coat. As I left our room, I told Kate that she would have to eat breakfast alone that morning. I told her that I had business to which to attend.

In the meantime McLaury and William Claiborne, a young punk who was out to make a name for himself with a gun, got together to talk.

Claiborne said that he had taken Ike Clanton to Dr. Charles Gillingham's office to have his head wound treated. They left to check up on Clanton. When they found him they all walked over to Spangenberg's Gun Shop behind Brown's Hotel. Now, on any other day, that would not have meant anything to anyone. But on this day, it meant plenty.

Moments later a group of miners stopped Virgil and asked, "Ain't you liable to have some trouble?"

One of them said, "I seen two more of them just rode in. Ike walked up to them and was telling them about your hitting him over the head with a six-shooter. One Cowboy said, 'Now is our time to make a fight.'"

Virgil, now convinced that the situation was more serious than he had originally thought, went over to the Wells, Fargo office to borrow a ten-gauge shotgun. By that time several groups of townsfolk had stopped on the street to speculate about just what was going on.

From his spot at Hafford's corner, Wyatt saw the Clanton bunch enter the gun shop and decided to check out what they were up to. He approached the shop, and, as he said later, "I saw them in the gun-shop changing cartridges into their belts." He added that he knew there was going to be trouble.

Virgil was still at the Wells, Fargo office when Bob Hatch peeked in to say, "For God's sake, get down there to the gun shop, for they are all down there and Wyatt is all alone. They are liable to kill him before you get there!"

Virgil ran down to the shop, just as Billy Clanton was filling his belt with cartridges. Wyatt calmed his brother's fears, and the two of them walked back to Hafford's corner, where they saw Tom McLaury, his head now bandaged, go into Everhardy's Eagle Market to take care of some business before catching up with the others, who had headed over to Dexter's Corral. As McLaury came out of Everhardy's, according to one observer, "his pants protruded as if there was a revolver" tucked inside his belt, and J. B. W Gardiner observed that he was sorry to see that Tom was now armed.

By that time, as you might well imagine, the citizens of Tombstone were alive with what was happening. Reality was a by-product of imagination, and everyone's imagination was working overtime. Several people came up to the Earps with various warnings about what the Cowboys were up to. One rumor placed Ike Clanton in the telegraph office, which Wyatt took to mean that he was summoning help. Meanwhile, Frank McLaury and Billy Clanton were convinced that the Earps were out to destroy them. The scene was set for disaster.

The only person in Tombstone who didn't seem to understand what was going on was Sheriff John H. Behan. He had strolled into Barron's Barber Shop for a shave, as he did every morning, when he was set upon by gossip about the situation. Once he left the shop, he ran into Charles Shibell, who had witnessed Virgil coldcock Ike earlier, and the two of them went off together to find the marshal. Along the way, they met Reuben Coleman, who told them that the Clantons and the McLaurys were up to no good. They were heavily armed and had crossed over Allen Street into the O.K. Corral, he said, advising Behan to "go and disarm that bunch!"

Coleman got to Virgil before Behan and Shibell did and repeated his warnings about the Cowboys. When the sheriff caught up to Virgil in a crowd of bystanders at Hafford's corner, Virg was clearly frustrated. Behan asked him what was going on, and Virgil snapped, "Some sons of bitches have been looking for a fight and now they can have it!"

"You had better disarm them," Behan said. "It is your duty as an officer."

"I will not. I will give them their chance to make a fight."

Wanting to avoid any disaster that might reflect poorly upon himself, Behan asked Virg into Hafford's Saloon for a drink. Virgil followed him in but declined his hospitality. As Behan downed the shot, William B. Murray, a local stockbroker and a leader of the Citizens Safety Committee, pulled the marshal aside and said, "I know you are going to have trouble and we have plenty of men and arms to assist you." Virgil, relieved to hear that he wasn't going up against the Cowboys alone, said, "As long as they stay in a corral, the O.K. Corral, I will not go down to disarm them. If they come out on the street, I will take their arms and arrest them."

"You can count on me if there is any danger," Murray promised before leaving.

Behan told Virgil that he was willing to go down to the corral and talk the Cowboys into laying down their arms. Anything, he said, was better than tempting a fight. Virg agreed, and Behan set off. As Virgil followed him out of the saloon, a Santa Fe railroad engineer stopped him and said that he had seen the Cowboys at the O.K. Corral and that he had overheard them threatening the Earps' lives. Probably he had heard Ike, all liquored up and tight, running off at the mouth. But each new allegation to reach the Earps added to what appeared to be a foregone conclusion: The Cowboys were out to get them. For good.

Now, by that time, I had finished my breakfast, still blissfully ignorant of what was transpiring, and walked over to the Alhambra Saloon to check on business. Morgan motioned me over and filled me in on the day's affairs. We walked together to Hafford's corner. As I approached Wyatt and Virgil, I asked Wyatt, "Where are you going?"

"We're going to make a fight," Wyatt said.

I looked at him somberly. "Well, you're not going to leave me out, are you?"

"This is none of your affair."

"That is a hell of a thing for you to say to me!" I said.

"It's going to be a tough one."

I looked him squarely in the eye and, squinting, said, "Tough ones are the kind I like."

Meanwhile Ike Clanton and Tom McLaury, upon being approached by John Behan, said that they were unarmed. Behan checked Ike to be sure. Tom McLaury pulled back the lapels of his coat to show that he was unarmed, but Behan confessed later that he "might have had a pistol and I did not know it."

Frank and Billy were both plainly armed, and Frank flatly refused to give up his weapon. He insisted that he did not want a fight, but he said he would not surrender his arms. Ike Clanton later testified, "Then Frank McLowry [*sic*] said he had business in town that he would like to attend to, but he would not lay aside his arms and attend to his business unless the Earps were disarmed."

Behan found himself in a quandary. Frank was obstinate, and Behan knew that his demand to disarm sworn peace officers was unreasonable.

As we waited impatiently for Behan's return, I looked across the faces of the Earps. They were, to a one, intense. Virgil was the eldest of the brothers, at thirty-eight, with Wyatt, who was thirty-three, Morgan, thirty, and me, the youngest of the group, also thirty—although four months younger than Morg. Suddenly Virg turned to me and asked if he could borrow my cane. I gladly surrendered it to him, and he handed me his ten-gauge, which I swung beneath my open coat.

After several more moments Virg motioned with his head toward the street, and the four of us—all standing about six feet tall and dressed impeccably in dark suits and coats—stepped down off the walk, turned, and began our trek very deliberately up Fourth Street. I could not help but think that my cane suited Virgil perfectly. It lent him an air of respectability. For what that was worth.

The negotiations between Behan and the Cowboys delayed things just long enough for our group to turn off Fourth Street onto Fremont. Someone yelled, "Here they come!"

Behan looked up and saw us walking briskly toward them. He said to the Clanton group, "I won't have no fighting, you must give me your firearms or leave town immediately."

"You need not be afraid, Johnny, we are not going to have any trouble," one of them replied. Behan accepted that statement, but he left the Cowboys still armed when he hurried up to confront Marshal Earp's party. As he approached I heard Virg say that if Behan demanded the shotgun, I was to let him have it.

"All right," I said.

Behan reached us just as we passed the market. With his hands outstretched, he urged, "Hold up boys! Don't go down there or there will be trouble."

Virgil stopped and stared him in the eye. "Johnny, I am going down to disarm them."

"I have been down there to disarm them," Behan replied.

The Earps looked from one to the other before picking up their pace again. Virgil appeared to be relieved; he tucked his pistol into his pants on his left hip and shifted my cane to his gun hand. Wyatt relaxed as well, slipping his own revolver into his overcoat pocket.

We instinctively suspected that Behan was lying.

We walked along for half a block, each of us staring straight ahead. I wanted to look over to Virg, to see what he was doing, to see if I could detect any discern in his face. My own hands were sweating, and my heart was beating more quickly than usual. Not out of fear or trepidation, not out of concern for the unknown, for I knew what lay before us. No, I was feeling alive, intense, *sharp*, focused, and in doing so my heightened senses drove me on. I stared straight ahead, to the intersection of Fourth and Fremont, wondering just how I would know when to turn, when to look to the side, how to know when Virg or Morg or Wyatt was making his move, if I would instinctively feel it or what. I had the unmistakable feeling of destiny on my shoulders, and I thought suddenly—so very briefly—about Kate, wondering if she had chosen to stay in our room or perhaps gotten out and gone to get something to eat. And then all thoughts of Kate left me, and my attention was focused on the job that lay ahead.

We walked resolutely toward the O.K. Corral in order, side by side. Our intent was to disarm Ike and Billy Clanton and the two McLaurys before they could do any more harm, realizing full well that the four Cowboys were just aching for a fight and would not surrender their guns peacefully.

And so it was that, around 2:30 p.m. on that chilly October afternoon, Marshal Virgil Earp, accompanied by deputies Wyatt and Morgan and John Henry Holliday, walked up Fourth Street, before turning onto Fremont, where we saw that the two Clantons and the two McLaurys had been joined by Billy Claiborne. They were standing in the vacant lot west of Fly's Boarding House. The five Cowboys, not realizing that I had left the building earlier, were lying in wait to catch me by surprise and to kill me. They obviously planned to make good on

Ike's threat. The cowardly way in which they had chosen to pull it off made me furious.

I moved out into the street apart from the rest of the Earp party. I knew that my role was one of backup, and I positioned myself accordingly to prevent any escape via the vacant lot or any attacks from the side. When Virgil turned in to the lot, he found Ike Clanton standing between the buildings. Along the side of the Harwood House stood the McLaury brothers and Billy Clanton. Two horses, Frank's and Billy's, both of which had "Winchester rifles in the saddle boots plainly in view," stood with the Cowboys.

Apparently, Clanton had walked away from the McLaurys to speak with Claiborne and handed the reins of his horse to Tom McLaury. As we approached, the kid stepped back against the wall alongside the McLaury brothers. He appeared nervous, but he was wearing a gun belt and a holstered revolver in clear violation of the law. Frank also had a pistol in plain view. We were caught off-guard by the sight of armed men and by the presence of Billy Claiborne and Wes Fuller, who had come to the corral too late to warn his friends that we were looking for them. At that point, Wyatt, observing the situation, mumbled something such as "Son-of-a-bitch" under his breath, contrary to later claims by the prosecution that Wyatt had used the expression as a threat.

I stood back and watched as Virgil moved into the lot toward Ike, with Wyatt following behind and Morgan hanging back on the sidewalk. He set himself in the street but moved closer to the center of the lot as Virgil stepped up and raised my cane in his right hand.

"Throw up your hands, boys. I intend to disarm you!"

"We will!" Frank McLaury called as he stepped forward and grabbed the revolver on his hip. Billy Clanton also reached for his gun, and Tom McLaury grabbed his coat lapels, peeling them back as if reaching for his draw. With Frank and Billy going for their pistols and none of the others obeying Virgil's order, Wyatt took no chances and pulled his own revolver. Within seconds I hoisted my shotgun into plain view from underneath my coat, pulling back the hammer of the sawed-off ten-gauge with an ominous *click*.

Virgil panicked. "Hold! I don't mean that," he shouted, as he stood waving my cane high above his head.

Wyatt's revolver exploded, just as McLaury's did, and the ball tore into Frank's gut just to the left of his navel, while Billy Clanton fired wide of Wyatt. Virgil shifted the cane to his other hand as he fumbled desperately to find the pistol on his hip, and the Cowboys froze as Frank stumbled from the impact of Wyatt's shot. I took a step toward Tom McLaury, who had shielded himself behind one of the horses. Ike Clanton suddenly charged Wyatt, grabbing him and wrestling with him before Wyatt shoved him away and growled, "The fight's commenced. Go to fighting or get away!"

Clanton broke and ran, stumbling through the door of Fly's and into a vacant lot, and then making his way through Kellogg's Saloon and into Toughnut Street before he stopped. In the flurry of gunfire that followed, both Ike Clanton and Billy Claiborne would later claim that the Earps shot at them, and the Earps believed that someone fired at them from just east of Fly's.

From my position I could see everything unfolding before me. Clanton took several quick bullets. I wheeled my gun in the general vicinity of Tom McLaury, who was brandishing his pistol in our direction, and railed a load of buckshot into his right arm and side. McLaury turned to run down Fremont Street, but before I could reload and fire again, he fell dead. Morg took a sudden shot to the right shoulder, the bullet penetrating his muscle, continuing through across his back, clipping his vertebrae, and exiting by his left shoulder.

Virg was shot suddenly in the right calf and had to struggle to keep his feet. Furious, I threw the shotgun down and drew my nickel-plated Colt from my pocket. Frank McLaury, clutching his stomach, shouted, "I've got you now," to which I replied, "You're a daisy if you have!"

I began emptying my slugs into McLaury right there in the middle of Fremont Street, and Morg fired several of his own into him. I felt a strike against my pistol pocket near my left hip and yelled, "I am shot right through!" I looked up to see Morgan fall to the ground. When McLaury tripped over backwards, I ran toward him. I heard Wyatt call out, "Watch out, Doc!" I yelled back, "The son of a bitch has shot me and I mean to kill him!" But McLaury was in his final death throes from a head wound beneath the right ear and a gut shot and died before I reached him.

And then everything fell suddenly ominously silent. Within mere seconds, months of tension that had built to a climax had erupted in a hailstorm of death. Both the McLaury brothers and Billy Clanton were dead. Ike Clanton and Billy Claiborne had cheated death by fleeing. Morg was wounded, and Virg as well, and I had been shot, too—although I did not know how seriously at the time.

Sheriff Behan reappeared. "I have to arrest you, Wyatt," he said.

"I won't be arrested," Wyatt said. He stared him right in the eyes. He stared him in the eyes and I thought for a moment he was going to draw on him. "You deceived me Johnny, you told me they were not armed. I won't be arrested. I am here to answer for what I've done. I am not going to leave town."

There was a tense moment before Sylvester Comstock, a local attorney and leader of Tombstone's Democratic Party, stepped in. "There is no hurry in arresting this man," he told Behan. "He done just right in killing them, and the people will uphold them."

"You bet we did right," Wyatt added. "We had to do it. And you threw us off, Johnny. You told us they were disarmed."

After the shootout, as the afternoon wind picked up and washed across Allen Street and past the open grounds of the corral, I looked at Wyatt, who was checking out his brother, Morg. I slipped my pistol back into my pocket, paused, and finally walked across the street, entering into Fly's Boarding House. When I got to our room, Kate asked me what had happened. I sat on the edge of the bed and cried.

"Oh," I said softly, "This is just awful—awful."

"Are you hurt?"

I looked up at her, into her face, and saw the genuine terror there. "No," I said, "I am not"; but when I removed my clothing, I saw a red streak two inches long across my hip where McLaury's bullet had grazed me.

And I knew I was the luckiest son of a bitch alive.

Later, an eyewitness to the entire affair recalled the event, short and sweet.

"Doc Holliday was hit in the left hip but kept on firing. Virgil Earp was hit in the third or fourth fire, in the leg, which staggered him but he kept up his effective work. Wyatt Earp stood up and fired in rapid succession, as cool as a cucumber, and was not hit. Doc Holliday was as calm as though at target practice and fired rapidly."

It was over as quickly as it had begun.

At the direction of the coroner, an inquest was held three days later, on October 29, at which the three Earp brothers and I were charged with the killings of Billy Clanton and Frank and Tom McLaury. Because of their wounds, Virgil and Morgan were spared the indignity of arrest. That was a pleasure Behan reserved solely for Wyatt and me, and Judge Wells Spicer set our bail at $10,000 apiece. We managed to raise our bonds and get out of jail pending the trial. But during the inquest, an attorney by the name of Will McLaury, who just happened to have been a brother to the two dead McLaurys, arrived in town from Texas. After gaining admittance to the Arizona bar, he made a motion in the courtroom to pressure Judge Spicer to revoke our bonds and return us to jail, and he issued a bench warrant for our arrests.

So, Behan arrested us again and turned us over to the court, and we were advised that we were being held without bail. Our attorney prepared a writ of habeas corpus dated November 7 and filed it in the court of Judge J. H. Lucas. The writ forced Judge Spicer to set a new bond. This time he settled upon a combined bail of $42,000 for the both of us. Although it took some doing, we eventually raised the funds, thanks to the generosity of friends and neighbors who were squarely on our side, including Wells, Fargo undercover agent Fred Dodge; Albert Billicke of the Cosmopolitan Hotel; William Hutchinson, who would go on to run the Birdcage Opera House; R. J. Winders, Wyatt's mining partner; and James Earp.

When the inquest finally began, each side asked the other probing questions designed to see if we had violated the law in acting as we had. After four weeks of testimony, Judge Spicer issued his ruling.

On November 29, 1881, Spicer said that Virgil Earp, acting in his capacity as chief of police, ". . . committed an injudicious and censurable act" in employing Wyatt, Morgan, and me to assist him in attempting to control the Clantons and the McLaurys. But he went beyond that, ultimately vindicating us all: "[A]lthough in this he [Virgil Earp] acted incautiously and without due circumspection, yet when we consider the conditions of affairs incident to a frontier country; the lawlessness and disregard for human life; the existence of a law-defying element in [our] midst; the fear and feeling of insecurity that has existed; the supposed prevalence of bad, desperate and reckless men who have been a terror to the country and kept away capital and enterprise; and consider the many threats that have been made against the Earps, I can attach no criminality to his unwise act. In fact, as the result plainly proves, he needed the assistance and support of staunch and true friends, upon whose courage, coolness and fidelity he could depend, in case of an emergency."

Spicer found that the Earp brothers and I had committed no offense in discharging our official duties.

Of course, the verdict outraged the Cowboys, who threatened to kill the Earps and me; and on December 12, 1881, acting territorial governor John J. Gosper telegraphed President Chester A. Arthur, informing him that armed troops were necessary in order to keep the peace in Tombstone. Talk on the street was that the Cowboys had earmarked a number of individuals for death. The Earps and I were high up on their list. I took that as a compliment.

Shortly thereafter I sent Kate back to the safety of the hotel in Globe, while the Earps and I took up more secure residence at the Cosmopolitan.

Over the course of the next several days, the political climate in Tombstone had taken a turn for the worse. The stage carrying the editor of the *Tombstone Epitaph* was fired upon. Justice Spicer received a message threatening his life if he failed to leave town. Several days later, late in the evening of December 28, somebody attempted to assassinate Virgil as he was crossing Fifth Street on his way back to his hotel room from the Oriental Saloon. Buckshot struck him in the back and in the left elbow, leaving his arm badly shattered, a condition that would mark him as permanently disabled. After the shooting, three men were observed running past the icehouse on Toughnut Street about a block away. Rumors had it that Will McLaury was behind a vengeful attack against the Earps and me. Using any means at their disposal, he, Ike Clanton, and Curly Bill Brocius had taken up a vendetta against us, most likely along with Hank Swilling and Frank Stilwell.

Our problems carried over into the new year, when Johnny Ringo and I confronted one another. On January 17, 1882, Ringo made some disparaging remarks about my backing the Earps, and I wouldn't hear of it. George Parsons wrote later in his diary, "Much bad blood in the air this afternoon. Ringo and Doc Holiday [*sic*] came nearly having it with pistols. . . . Bad time expected with the Cowboy leader and D. H. I passed both not knowing blood was up. One with hand in breast pocket and the other probably ready."

Later Parsons added, "I heard the latter [Holliday] say 'All I want of you is ten paces out in the street.' A few paces away was Wyatt, and across the street was a man with a rifle watching proceedings. The stage was complete for an encounter, but it did not come off at that time."

James Flynn, who had been named the town's new chief of police to replace the injured Virgil, stepped in between us, and we were both arrested for carrying weapons within the town limits. We appeared before Judge Albert Wallace and were each fined $30.

But that was not the end of any bad blood between us. In fact, it was only the beginning.

A Shot in the Dark

THE DEADLY BULLET

Tombstone Daily Epitaph, *March 20, 1882*

THE ASSASSIN AT LAST SUCCESSFUL IN HIS DEVILISH MISSION. MORGAN EARP SHOT DOWN AND KILLED WHILE PLAYING BILLIARDS

At 10:00 Saturday night while engaged in playing a game of billiards in Campbell & Hatch's Billiard Parlor, on Allen between Fourth and Fifth, Morgan Earp was shot through the body by an unknown assassin. At the time the shot was fired he was playing a game with Bob Hatch, one of the proprietors of the house who was standing with his back to the glass door in the rear of the room that opens out upon the alley that leads straight through the block along the west side of A. D. Otis & Co.'s store to Fremont Street. This door is the ordinary glass door with four panes in the top in place of panels. The two lower panes are painted, the upper ones being clear. Anyone standing outside can look over the painted glass and see everything going on in the room just as well as though standing in the open door. At the time the shot was fired, the deceased must have been standing within ten feet of the door, and the assassin standing near enough to see his position, took aim for the middle of his person, shooting through the upper portion of the whitened glass. The bullet entered the right side of the abdomen, passing through the spinal column, completely shattering it, emerging on the left side, passing the length of the room and lodging in the thigh of Geo. A. B. Berry, who was standing by the stove, inflicting a painful flesh wound.

Instantly after the first shot a second was fired through the top of the upper glass which passed across the room and lodged in the wall near the ceiling over the head of Wyatt Earp, who was sitting as a spectator of the game. Morgan fell instantly upon the first fire and lived only one hour. His brother Wyatt, Tipton, and McMasters rushed to the side of the wounded man and tenderly picked him up and moved him some ten feet away near the door of the card room, where Drs. Matthews, Goodfellow and Millar, who were called, examined him and, after a brief consultation, pronounced the wound mortal. He was then moved into the card room and placed on the lounge where in a few brief moments he breathed his last, surrounded by his brothers, Wyatt, Virgil, James and Warren with the wives of Virgil and James and a few of his most intimate friends. Notwithstanding the intensity of his mortal agony, not a word of complaint escaped his lips, except when they tried to move him to the doctor's office to provide him better care. "Don't," he cried out. "I can't stand it." Settling back into the lounge, he looked up at Hatch and said, "I have played my last game of pool."

The funeral cortege started away from the Cosmopolitan hotel about 12:30 yesterday with the fire bell tolling its solemn peals of "Earth to earth, dust to dust."

It hurts to this day to think about the loss of such a fine young man. In many ways, I felt closest to him of all the Earp boys. I respected Wyatt the most, you understand. He was a very special, very courageous, and very intelligent man. But I liked the others to a one. They were like a bunch of overgrown children. Morgan, most of all. He was always ready to laugh, always eager to seek out a good time and usually find it, often at the expense of his brothers. Morgan was the younger brother I never had and always wanted. Or maybe he was the reincarnation of my cousin Robert. Whatever he was, God, how I missed him.

I remember the entire sordid affair as if it had happened only last night. On that fateful evening a play was scheduled at Scheifflin Hall on Fourth Street, across from the County Courthouse. The handbill for the play, which was called *Stolen Kisses* or something to that effect, proclaimed "Two Hours of Incessant Laughter." How could Morg resist?

Of course, we had already gotten word that there might be trouble that evening, following on the heels of the shootings at the Corral, but none of us took that very seriously. It seemed that the theater was as safe a place to be as anywhere, amongst all the people in attendance; so when Morg asked me if I wanted to join Dan Tipton and him, I accepted readily.

On the way to our seats, we ran into a legal mouthpiece whom the Cowboys on occasion used in their scrapes with the law. His name was Briggs Goodrich, and for some reason he took Morg to one side and warned him, "You fellows will catch it tonight if you don't look out." Well, we all three of us—and Wyatt, as well—had been listening to the braggadocio from Ike Clanton and Frank Stilwell and Indian Charlie and the rest for months. They were still upset about the killings, as well as the Earps' general willingness to stand up to them and hold them accountable for their nefarious deeds committed before and after we had met them for the showdown at the Corral. To me, it seemed as if it was just another attempt to ruin our day, to cause us undue concern, especially since Johnny Ringo had promised earlier that, if any trouble started, he was going to stay out of it and look after himself. Without Ringo backing their play, it was unlikely that they would try any rough stuff.

So we sat through the production, which I found to be generally amusing and which Morg licked up like molasses off a biscuit, and when it was over, he and Tipton said they were going down to the billiard parlor to shoot a game or two with Bob Hatch and asked if I wanted to come along. The Earps had pretty much made Campbell & Hatch's their headquarters since Wyatt had sold his share of ownership in the Oriental.

But I was a little tired that evening and a sort under the weather, the cussed coughing and wheezing, and about all I could think of was a glass of whiskey to calm me down and a quiet night's sleep. My whore was out of town wenching and rooting around for more money than she could generally have expected to wrangle out of the locals, so I had no reason not to turn in.

After I took off my gun and laid it atop the chifforobe, I grabbed a bottle of rye, having denuded myself of the bourbon earlier in the day, and filled it to within a finger of the rim. I had barely emptied the glass and laid myself out on the bed when I heard two shots in quick succession.

Fearing the worst—that the Cowboys had finally followed through on one of their cowardly threats—I grabbed my coat and belt and bolted from the room, down two flights of steps, and out into the street where I saw people congregating outside the billiard parlor three doors down.

"Oh, my God," I said half to myself and took off on a dead run.

When I reached the front door, I shoved my way past some people blocking the entry and stopped cold. I looked past the table closest to the back of the room and saw my friend Wyatt hunched down on the floor, saw the blood, and knew in a heartbeat what had happened. And then, as I rushed up to him, I realized I'd been wrong. It wasn't Wyatt who had been shot at all, but Morg.

As I bent down beside him, Wyatt looked up at me with deep, soulful, swollen eyes, eyes begging for release. Old Doc Millar suddenly forced his way into the room, with Doc Goodfellow behind him, and Millar stooped down to check on Morg, who was still conscious and losing blood fast, while Goodfellow rushed over to where George Berry, a mine employee who had come in to warm himself by the stove, was clutching his thigh.

"Is he going to be all right, doc?" Wyatt asked. Morg had been shot in the side, and from the angle of the bullet's entry, I knew it did not look good. Millar only shook his head.

"Let's get him up off the floor," the doctor said. "A couple of you men, help me out here. Let's get him into the back room." Wyatt and two of his friends got their hands positioned beneath his legs and back, and as they lifted him in unison, Morg let out a sharp yelp.

"Easy, Morg," I told him. "You're going to be all right." But I saw from the look on his face that he knew differently.

As Virgil, James, and Warren rushed into the room, the two Earp wives right behind them, they stopped cold at the sight. Somebody said to go get Mattie, *fast,* and I grabbed Wyatt's arm. My compatriot looked up at me again.

"Who did it?" I asked.

He said not a word, but his eyes spoke loud and clear. I felt the pain in my heart tear away at me, rip away my vitals from the inside, rip no less cursedly than the young man sprawled out before us had been ripped from his very life, and the tears began trickling from my eyes. I squeezed Wyatt's arm and felt him go limp. He turned back to Morgan, who said something to him so softly that Wyatt had to lean close to hear. The doctor asked if Morg thought he could be moved to his office, where he could better be taken care of, but when they tried to get him to his feet, he cried softly to leave him be.

After Goodfellow had finished tending to Barry's wound, he came over to assist Millar and a third doctor who had by then joined in the fray. Millar turned to Wyatt and said softly that there was nothing they could do. The wound was fatal.

At first Wyatt didn't seem to understand the words . . . or *wouldn't,* I was not quite sure which. I think I may have bent down to tell Morgan to hold on, that I would get him something for the pain, and I swear that I saw his two lips curl up at the corners, as if trying to smile. Bob Hatch moved closer to the man to tell him something, but Morg raised the first three fingers on his left hand and whispered softly, "This is the last game of pool I'll ever play."

By that time the billiard parlor had filled with people, and someone yelled out, "They got clean away!" I turned to Wyatt and put my arm around his shoulders. And as Morgan Earp clung tentatively to the last few moments of life on earth, I said to him, "Don't bet on it," and Wyatt turned to me and began to weep.

When his wife, Mattie, came to console him, I slowly rose, the anger within my soul rising with me. I felt suddenly crazed. I pushed through the crowd, stormed out of the building and down the street, and began kicking in the doors of private homes, looking for attorney Will McLaury and Sheriff Johnny Behan, believing that they were responsible for the murder of my good, kind, and fun-loving friend. I would've killed them both had I found them.

Fortunately for me, I hadn't.

The next morning, Sunday, was Wyatt's thirty-fourth birthday. After having endured a short and fitful sleep, I came upon him emerging from the hotel. We glanced at one another and knew in an instant what had to be done. It is the code of the South, the antebellum code of honor. When the law fails to provide justice, the man steps forth.

"I ache for you, Wyatt," I told him as we walked along in the general direction of the marshal's office. "He was in many ways like my own brother."

"Yes," Wyatt said. "I know he was."

"I'm going to miss him. Everyone is going to miss him."

"Yes," Wyatt said. We stopped, and he faced me. "Doc, we're going to send Morg's body to Contention and place him on the train for California. I'm sending Virg and Allie home, too. Morg's wife Lou will meet them at Colton and make the final arrangements."

"I think that is the wise thing to do," I told him.

"I'm sending Nellie and Mattie back with them as well."

"How about James and Warren?"

He paused. "James and Warren are staying here with me. I have some work to do. I'm going to be busy, and I'm going to need their help."

I pulled a flask from my hip pocket, unscrewed the cap, and drank in deeply. I offered it to Wyatt, who shook it off. "What about me?" I asked.

Wyatt shook his head. "This ain't your fight, Doc. Not this time."

I placed the flask back in my pocket and turned toward him, his eyes squinting from the early morning sun or from the steely glint of determination he found in mine, I'm not sure. "That's a helluva thing to say to me," I said.

He seemed to breathe in deeply, and we turned and continued on our way.

Later that morning the coroner held an inquest to investigate Morg's death. Mrs. Marietta Spencer testified that late the night before, her husband, Pete, returned home in the company of Frank Stilwell, Indian Charlie Florentino Cruz, and John Doe Freis. This had been only an hour or so after Morgan had been shot. Mrs. Spencer also testified that before coming to the inquest, her husband had threatened her with violence if she related to the court what she knew. In direct defiance she stated under oath that she believed her husband and Frank Stilwell had killed Morgan Earp with help from Indian Charlie.

The following Sunday Wyatt and I joined the funeral procession carrying Morg's body to the train depot in Contention. I had requested that he be attired in one of my finest tailored suits, and the undertaker fitted him accordingly. Wyatt told me he blamed the entire Cowboy faction for his brother's murder. And I could see in his eyes that he was telling the truth. Of course, I fully agreed with him and swore right then and there my allegiance in the vendetta that would ultimately result in the deaths of Stilwell, Indian Charlie, Curly Bill Brocius, Johnny Barnes, and that cur of a scoundrel, Johnny Ringo.

As we readied ourselves for the trip, Wyatt received word that Frank Stilwell, Ike Clanton, and two other Cowboys were watching every train that entered the yard with the intent to ambush and kill Virgil Earp and his wife. Wyatt decided that we needed to accompany them to Tucson to make sure that they boarded safely for California.

And as I thought about what lay ahead for us all, I thought, too, about the words that Wyatt had once told me Judge Stilwell had imparted to him. Words that now rang so true.

"Leave your prisoners out in the brush where alibis don't count."

Rough Riders

Before we had embarked upon our own vendetta to avenge the cowardly murder of Morgan Earp, Wyatt had to arrange for his brother's body to be transported to the Earp family home near Colton, California, just west of Los Angeles. He had also planned on transporting the wounded Virgil and his wife, Allie, along with Mattie and Morgan's widow, Lou, out of Tombstone. It was no longer safe for any of the Earps, or me, to remain behind. I felt that Kate was out of danger at the hotel back in Globe. I thanked God that at least I hadn't her to worry about.

So, even before the coroner's inquest had begun, Wyatt, his brother Warren, Turkey Creek Jack Johnson, Sherman McMasters, and I left the Cosmopolitan Hotel. It was Sunday, March 19, 1882. Wyatt, who still recognized himself as a duly deputized officer of the law, took his newly formed posse, and we escorted the wounded Virgil, the Earp wives, and Morgan's lifeless body north to Contention, where we boarded a train for Tucson. From there, our plan was to have Virgil and the wives accompany Morgan's casket on another train heading toward the Earps' family home in California. James and Bessie Earp, along with Wyatt's wife, Mattie, boarded the next train headed west.

Although we didn't know it at the time, Frank Stilwell, one of the murderers of Morg Earp, had taken an earlier train to Tucson. Stilwell was scheduled to appear before a grand jury there on charges of robbing the United States mail in the Bisbee stage holdup that previous September.

Shortly after seven o'clock that Monday evening, we pulled into the train depot in Tucson. Wyatt had been tipped off that Ike Clanton and Stilwell had gotten word that we were coming and had preceded us to town. After having dinner at the hotel across from the station, Wyatt excused himself to take a look around the yard. He had learned that several men had been seen lying on a flatcar near the engine. Wyatt had seen them, too, and recognized one of them as Stilwell, the man he was convinced had killed his brother. He recognized another as Ike Clanton.

As the train prepared to depart, Wyatt slipped away quietly. By the time I had caught up with him, Stilwell was dead. Wyatt had run him down and shot him—unloading both barrels into him as he lay quivering, begging for mercy. Warren, McMasters, and Creek Johnson caught up with us at about the same time, and within moments a volley of gunfire exploded, riddling the body of the fallen Cowboy beyond recognition.

Wyatt flashed a sign to Virgil as the train began its solitary journey west. *One down,* he signaled.

The following morning a trackman for the Southern Pacific Railroad discovered the bullet-riddled body of Frank Stilwell lying face up alongside the tracks. He'd been shot numerous times. He'd been shot numerous times by Wyatt Earp. He'd been shot numerous times by me, and he'd been shot by everybody else who was with us because they hated everything that Frank Stilwell ever stood for. We had unloaded our lead into him that night, just as we had unloaded our frustrations and our remorse over our lost brother's life until there was nothing more to unload.

Wyatt's posse returned to Tombstone on March 21, when Sheriff Behan informed us that warrants had been issued for the arrest of one Wyatt Earp and Doctor John Henry Holliday. We were handed the warrants and refused to accept them. We had every right to do so. Tombstone Mayor John Carr had told Behan that Judge William H. Stilwell of the District Court had entrusted Wyatt and his posse with the job of arresting people for diverse criminal offenses that had occurred during the course of the past several months. By that court order, Wyatt was totally vindicated in riding the Revenge Trail—and taking a great deal of personal pleasure in the experience. After all, the code of the West took precedence over the laws of mere mortals. We had "right" on our side.

Behan did not take our refusal lightly. He went around town, deputizing the area's most notorious men, all of whom just happened to be enemies of the Tombstone Earps and me, to assist in arresting us. Included in Behan's newly deputized posse were none other than Ike Clanton and Johnny Ringo.

We knew, of course, that we were in trouble, because now not only did we have the Cowboy mob after us, but they were acting, at Behan's bequest, as a legal posse. We decided the best thing to do for our own sake was to leave Tombstone as quickly as possible.

So we left. Wyatt, Sherman McMasters, Turkey Creek Johnson, Texas Jack Vermilion, and me—we all left together, the day after Stilwell's body had been discovered in Tucson. We rode out that morning to Pete Spencer's wood camp in the South Pass of the Dragoon Mountains, hoping to find Spencer and Indian Charlie.

We did.

The following morning the body of Indian Charlie, riddled with bullets, was discovered alongside the trail. The day after that news surfaced that the body of Curly Bill Brocius had been found near Iron Springs in the Whetstone Mountains. Johnny Barnes admitted before he died from wounds incurred in the same fight that they had been jumped by a band of desperados bent upon revenge.

Interestingly enough, once the shooting had begun, everyone turned his horse and headed for cover, yours truly included. Everyone, that is, except Wyatt. He jumped off his mount, stood his ground, and continued coolly pumping iron into the murderers' lair. He grabbed a shotgun from his horse as someone shouted for Curly Bill, and he opened fire, cutting the man nearly in half. Finally, after forty or fifty shots had been returned, Wyatt grabbed his horse and proceeded to remount as lead flew all around him. When he finally caught up with us, I rode up to him, fully expecting him to be shot to hell. Everyone, including Wyatt, thought he had been shot, and we were amazed to find otherwise. There were bullet holes in his saddle, and his coat was shredded, but not a mark on him. I think we would have all been killed if God Almighty wasn't on our side.

We spent that night camping in the Whetstones. The next morning, Dan Tipton, who brought both news and money from Tombstone, joined us on our way to Dragoon Summit, where we flagged down an eastbound train on the afternoon of March 26. After searching every car we got back off and continued on toward the mountains. We had dinner that day at Henderson's ranch before camping in a grassy knoll one mile to the north.

At daybreak on the morning of March 27, we left camp and proceeded north to Colonel Henry C. Hooker's Sierra Bonita Ranch in Graham County. The colonel was a true Southern gentleman of marked upbringing who showed us proper hospitality and gave us food and feed for our horses. The details of this portion of our journey somehow managed to make themselves known, in a letter dated April 4, 1882, in the *Tombstone Epitaph*. It was signed only "One of Them," and it said simply, "Next morning, not being in a hurry to break our camp, our stay was long enough to notice the movements of Sheriff Behan and his posse of honest ranchers, with whom, if they had possessed the trailing abilities of an average Arizona ranch man, we might have had trouble, which we are not seeking." The letter continued with its reference to the hot trail that the Earp and Holliday party was following on the heels of Charlie Ross.

"We are confident that our trailing abilities will soon enable us to turn over to the gentlemen the fruits of our efforts so that they may not again return to Tombstone empty-handed."

Although we never got to see that letter published in the newspaper because of our hard ride north toward New Mexico by way of Cedar

Springs Road to the Gila River, I know for a fact that it existed. I know for a fact, because I wrote it. And I sent it.

Yet, despite our successes on the trail, things had somehow managed to take a serious turn for the worse. It was not an unusual state of affairs for me in my life at the time. In fact, I was beginning to get used to it. I was beginning to enjoy it, the challenge of having brick walls erected suddenly in my path, only to have to figure out a way to crash through them, or work my way around them.

Wyatt came up to me and asked if I wanted to back out of the fray. He had observed my worsening physical condition and expressed some concerns about it, and I'm sure that was what was behind his thinking. I told him, "Why Wyatt, I am shocked to hear of such a thing. I have told you that I would be with you to my dying day. And I meant it. It was an oath. I cannot take it back."

Wyatt looked at me with those cold steel-blue eyes of his and said, "Doc, I know that. I just thought I had to make the offer."

So, on April 7, 1882, the Earps and the rest of our group arrived in Silver City, New Mexico Territory. We had done everything in our power to keep our activities quiet. We were successful. It wasn't until several days after we had left that the *New Southwest and Grand County Herald* published the following newspaper story.

> Last Saturday evening at 10 o'clock, the Earp boys' party and Doc Holliday were in Silver City. They went at once to the Exchange Hotel to find the stage agent to make arrangements to leave the next morning on the Deming coach. They slept in a private house uptown and took breakfast the next morning in the Broadway restaurant, as they had not registered at any hotel, it was not known they were in town until after their departure. The party came on horseback, and put up with the Elephant Corral. They were all mounted and armed to the teeth. One of the men when asked his name, he answered John Smith, and another Bill Snooks. This excited the suspicion of Mr. White, proprietor of the Corral, and the next morning

when they offered to sell him their horses, he refused to buy them, fearing to get himself in trouble. They offered six of their horses for $300, but as the horses were worth more than that, this offer was also looked on as unfavorable to them. They finally sold the six horses to Mr. Miller, who is about to start a livery stable here.

After riding the stage to Fort Cummings, we boarded the Santa Fe Railroad at nearby Deming. From Deming, we traveled through Socorro to Albuquerque, where we remained about ten days with Frank McLane, a close friend of Wyatt's from Dodge City, who loaned us $2,000.

Once again aboard the train, the seven of us traveled through Las Vegas and into the new state of Colorado, disembarking near Trinidad, in the small town of El Moro. We spent several days there with Bat Masterson, who had become the city marshal. Then we decided to separate. Our work was complete.

McMasters and Johnson split from the group and ended up in Utah. Vermillion's path led him to Virginia. Before continuing on, we divided the $2,000 amongst us. Around May 7, I arrived in Pueblo, aboard the Denver and Rio Grande Railroad. The Earps and Tipton left Trinidad for Gunnison, Colorado, where they set up a secret camp outside of town near a local ranch. We were still on the run not only from the Cowboys but also from Johnny Behan, who we were sure had a warrant out for our arrest in Arizona. Although I had pledged my support to Wyatt and his brothers, I had a bad feeling about it all.

Shortly after I arrived in Pueblo, secure in the belief that I had safely escaped the wrath of the vindictive bad men of Arizona, I paid a visit to Tom Kemp's Comique Variety Theatre. There, a man by the name of Perry M. Mallen introduced himself to me and said that I had once saved his life in Santa Fe, New Mexico. He said that he felt obligated to tell me that Stilwell's brother was in Pueblo in order to avenge his brother Frank's death. I told him he must have been mistaken, since I had never been in Santa Fe in my life. Nevertheless, I thanked him for the information about Stilwell and promptly forgot about the incident.

On May 8, back in Tombstone, the old case against me in my fight with Milt Joyce was called before Judge William H. Stilwell. When I failed to appear, the court declared my bond forfeited and closed the books on the case.

I had anticipated that, of course, and was not about to return to Tombstone and John Behan's group of cutthroats for any amount of love or money. Instead, on Sunday, May 14, I joined Bat Masterson, Sam Osgood, and a fellow whom I had known only as Texas George, and we left Pueblo to attend the races scheduled for the following Tuesday in Denver. Afterward, I planned on putting still more distance between the Cowboys and me by moving on toward Wood River country.

Around nine o'clock the following Monday evening, I was walking back to our hotel after dinner when I heard a familiar voice behind me call out my name. I turned to find Mallen, who was holding on me and ordered me to throw up my hands because I was under arrest. At first I thought he was joking, but then Mallen said that he was a Los Angeles County deputy sheriff and that he had a warrant for my arrest for the murder of Frank Stilwell. After a small crowd had gathered, we walked to the nearby sheriff's office, where a wagon was summoned to take me to the county jail.

It was all beginning to make sense, in a strange sort of way. Mallen was a paid mercenary sent by John Behan and his cohorts in Tombstone. Behan couldn't wait to get me back to Arizona to turn me over into the clutches of the Cowboys, particularly after the Earps and I had eluded arrest so smoothly earlier. Now, apparently, he was getting serious.

From my cell, I managed to get word to Marshal Masterson about what had transpired. Masterson, with the aid of Denver attorney Frank A. Naylor of the law firm of Naylor and Richardson, set out to secure a writ of habeas corpus. At 3:30 that morning, District Judge Victor A. Elliott signed the writ and ordered Arapahoe County Sheriff Michael Spangler to bring me for an appearance before the court later that day.

All the local newspapers, as well as a few in nearby Arizona, treated the arrest as if it were major news. You would have thought they had captured the anti-Christ, himself! Although a few papers ran articles in my support, denouncing the activities of the Cowboys and the allegiance of the Behan faction, others portrayed me as a cold-blooded gunfighter and a murderer who deserved to be behind bars—or worse! I thought it particularly comforting that, to a one, they described me as a handsome gentleman of a tall, slender stature with a sophisticated, soft-spoken manner and piercing blue eyes. I always liked that "piercing blue eyes" part.

Of my appearance, the *Denver Republican* wrote, "His features are well-formed. And there is a . . . well-defined look of determination from his eyes. . . . Holliday was dressed neatly in black, with a colored linen shirt. The first thing noticeable about him in opening the conversation was his soft voice and modest manner."

The *Pueblo Daily Chieftain* stated on May 17, 1882, that "Doc Holliday is a man of light weight, rather tall, smoothly shaven, and is always well-dressed. Streaks of gray can be seen in his hair . . . His eyes are blue, large, sharp and piercing. He is not over thirty five years of age, and as straight as an arrow. He is well educated, and his conversation shows him to be a man of considerable culture." Later that day Denver's *Rocky Mountain News* confirmed to my edification that "Holladay [sic] is a delicate, gentlemanly-looking man, slightly built and with prematurely gray hair. He wears a heavy sandy mustache."

While I waited for my release from jail, I learned that Mallen had been making the rounds, boasting that he had been in hot pursuit of me for the past seven years. He said I had murdered Mallen's friend Harry White in Utah, and that I had led him on a chase that involved cattle theft, stage robbery, and many more killings. While Mallen's exaggerations were promptly eaten up by the local reporters, I quietly set about correcting the record. I had never been to Utah and had never robbed a stage, I told one reporter. Mallen's warrant was obviously phony because Frank Stilwell had been killed in Pima County, while the warrant was from Cochise County. I told anyone who would listen that Mallen's charges were simply a plot to return me to Arizona, where I was sure I would have met my own violent death at the hands of the Cowboys.

I went on to explain to the *Denver Republican*, "We hunted the rustlers, and they all hate us. John Behan, Sheriff of Cochise County, is one of the gang, and a deadly enemy of mine, who would give any money to have me killed. It is all certain that he instigated the assassination of Morgan Earpp [*sic*]. Should he get me in his power my life would not be worth much."

A number of the town's most respectable citizens came to my defense. Bat Masterson, for one, said, "I tell you all of this talk is wrong about Holliday. I know him well. He is a dentist and a good one." Masterson went on to say that Mallen was a fraud and a "friend of the Cowboys, whose only object is to get Holliday back [to Arizona Territory] in order that he might be killed."

Another man coming to my defense was Lee Smith, an old friend of the Holliday family from Georgia days long since passed. Smith had owned a liquor and tobacco store in Griffin and had known most of my family for much of his life. He later became an investment banker and was at that time living in Denver in order to watch over his gold mines. Smith met with me at the jail and assured me that he would help me in any way possible. He said that he would soon be traveling back to Atlanta, and he promised to contact Dr. John S. Holliday to ensure that he would hear the truth about this entire ordeal, and not merely the fanciful conjecture concocted by the local gossips. Smith also promised to meet with Governor Frederick W. Pitkin in an effort to persuade him to step in on my behalf.

Sometime later, in granting an interview to the *Atlanta-Post Appeal*, Lee Smith described me as "one of the best boys that ever lived, if he is left alone, but you mustn't impose upon him or you will smell burning powder."

On Wednesday, May 17, I received another surprise in the form of a warrant charging me with operating a confidence game that had resulted in the loss of $150 by my victim. The next day City Marshal

Henry Jamieson of Pueblo walked into Sheriff Spangler's office with the warrant, seeking my custody. It was a charge brilliantly conceived by Masterson and several other of my loyal friends in order to keep me safe from the Cowboys' vendetta in the event that I were released under the writ. The court withheld granting Jamieson custody of me until after the habeas corpus hearing.

While I sat in jail awaiting my future, Sheriff Behan in Tombstone received a notice from the office of Arizona Governor Frederick A. Tritle, refusing to issue a request to Colorado seeking my extradition because the warrant had been issued by a county other than the one in which the murder of Stilwell had occurred. Never one to miss an opportunity, Behan contacted Pima County Sheriff Bob Paul and requested that a new warrant be issued from his county, along with yet another requisition from the governor for my return to Arizona. After granting Behan's request, Paul realized that he had made a mistake and that arresting me and returning me to Arizona would be contradictory to my future health and prosperity. He quickly left for Colorado to oversee personally my extradition back to the Territory.

My friends in Colorado all agreed with Sheriff Paul, knowing that if I were extradited to Arizona, the Cowboys would never allow me to see the light of another day. Paul arrived in Denver on Friday, May 19, with the properly issued warrant in hand, but did not have the requisition from Governor Tritle to take custody of me and remove me from the state.

The following Monday, Judge Elliott postponed a hearing on the writ of habeas corpus until the next day, hoping to receive the governor's requisition before having to make a ruling. On Tuesday morning at 10 o'clock, he surprised everybody when he discharged the case after learning that Perry Mallen had admitted his entire story to be nothing more than a hoax.

Of course, for whatever the reason, I was ecstatic to be free. But my ecstasy quickly turned to dismay when Deputy Sheriff Charles T. Linton quickly rearrested me, this time under the actual original warrant issued by Sheriff Paul. My attorneys promptly applied for a second writ of habeas corpus to keep me from having to return to Arizona, and another hearing was scheduled for that coming Friday. Until then, I was to remain in jail.

The requisition from Governor Tritle of the Arizona Territory reached Sheriff Paul in Denver two days later, on Thursday, May 24. Paul presented it to Colorado Governor Pitkin, who "took it under advisement." After yet another delay, on Monday, May 29, all of the concerned parties, including Pitkin, gathered in Judge Elliott's courtroom to hear arguments from the Honorable Isaac E. Barnum on behalf of the authorities, plus Judge Westbrook S. Decker and Colonel John T. Deweese, acting as my personal legal representatives. It is fairly common knowledge that the governor had already received private testimony on my behalf from some of my staunchest friends and allies.

In the end Pitkin decided that the Arizona requisition had failed to provide sufficient authentication of the issued warrant. In addition, since another outstanding warrant existed in Pueblo, the state of Colorado had priority over Arizona in holding me in custody. Judge Elliott released me in order to present Pueblo with the opportunity to exercise its warrant, which it did. I was arrested again on the spot by Pueblo City Marshal Jamieson on the outstanding warrant, this one charging me with larceny.

Accompanied by Bat Masterson and Sheriff Paul, I made the trip to Pueblo. Paul said that he wanted to go along for my protection in the event that Pueblo authorities released me. In the meantime Mallen, who had started this entire ruckus, admitted that he was not in actuality a sheriff from Los Angeles, that he had lied about having spent the past seven years in my pursuit, and that he was actually a bounty hunter in search of the reward money offered on my head by John Behan back in Tombstone. As if that weren't enough, Mallen—authorities soon enough learned—had defrauded several Denver residents of several hundred dollars before quietly slipping out of town.

So, on Wednesday, May 31, Masterson, Paul, Deputy Sheriff Linton, and I all arrived in Pueblo on the morning train. That same afternoon I appeared before Justice McBride on a charge of larceny for having fraudulently obtained funds from Charles White of Pennsylvania. The case was presented to the July term of the District Court, and I was released on $300 bail.

The local papers, of course, had a picnic with all the news about the onetime dentist from Georgia turned gunfighter and murderer in the Wild West. I had become something of an instant celebrity, and I took every advantage of my newly created status to exclaim to the press that I was innocent of being a bunko man—or of practically any other crimes you could name.

Several days after my release on bail, Wyatt had granted a street-side interview with a reporter from the *Gunnison News–Democrat*. He told him that I would be joining his brother and him in Gunnison. He spoke about the death of Curly Bill. When the reporter asked if I had killed Frank Stilwell, Wyatt replied, "Well, Stillwell [*sic*] was killed at Tucson." At least, he added, that's what he had been led to believe. He quickly changed the subject. "I promised my brother [Morgan] to get even, and I've kept my word so far. When they shot him, he said that the only thing he regretted was that he wouldn't have a chance to get even. I told him I'd attend to it for him."

The Pueblo newspaper reported in a story on June 14 that I was still in town awaiting action from the grand jury. But by June 16, I had arrived in Gunnison and reunited with the Earps. There, a news reporter approached me, writing later, "[He was] dressed in a dark close-fitting suit of black, and wore the latest style of round top hat. His hair was seen to be quite gray, his mustache sandy, and his eyes a piercing dark blue." I later told one reporter, "I'm not traveling about the country in search of notoriety, and I think you newspaper fellows have already had a fair hack at me." Nevertheless, I answered all of their questions: I was born in Georgia, educated at the Pennsylvania College of Dental Surgery, and practiced dentistry in Texas. I admitted to having been a member of the Methodist church there, as well as belonging to a temperance organization, and I explained that I had also lived in Fort Griffin and Dennison as well as in Denver in 1875 and 1876. I concluded the interview by saying that my intention was to mind my own business and "let other people do the same."

That was only one of many interviews, news articles, and reported sightings of Wyatt Earp, Warren Earp, and me over the course of the next several days. We *wanted* to be noticed and have our whereabouts firmly established in case they might come under scrutiny later in a court of law. We were not about to make the same mistake we had made with the killing of Frank Stilwell. One Leadville, Colorado, newspaper reported that I was in Gunnison on July 1. A news item in the *Salida Mountain Mail* dated July 8, 1882, reported that I had arrived in town the day before and made it known that I planned to stay for a while.

About that time the newspaper stories fell strangely silent, as I slipped quietly out of town to join Wyatt, Warren, and Dan Tipton, who were waiting for me just outside the Salida, Colorado, town limits. From there, we rode south together in search of another of Morgan's assassins, Johnny Ringo. We traversed Poncha Pass before turning up San Luis Creek for the seventy-five-mile trek to Alamosa. There, we boarded the train to Espanola before continuing on to Santa Fe, where we boarded the trunk line to Lamy. We finally arrived in the Lordsburg area on July 10 or 11.

On July 11, back in Pueblo County, Colorado, the court had just issued a writ of *capias* for me, stating that I had not been present in court and that the sheriff of Pueblo County should advise me that my bail was being reset at $500. Later that day attorney W. G. Hollands learned of the writ and appeared before the court on my behalf, which seemed to satisfy the judge.

Meanwhile, on Sunday, July 9, Johnny Ringo was holed up at the Cowboys' hangout near Galeyville. He had been drinking pretty heavily, as he was known to do. By Thursday morning, July 13, a man named Bill Sanders, whose ranch was at the mouth of Turkey Creek Canyon, passed a drunken Ringo wandering along the nearby string of watering holes called the Tanks. Later that day Mrs. Will Smith, who lived near the mouth of neighboring Morse Canyon, heard a single gunshot.

Sometime thereafter, John Yoast, a local teamster, showed up at the Smith house and informed the woman that, while he'd been hauling lumber down from the canyon, he had stumbled across the dead body of John Ringo. Apparently, he had shot himself—or somebody else had—in the head. His body had been found at a spot below the Smith Ranch along the road into Morse Canyon. If anyone else were involved, they had quickly dispersed from the area. There had been no witnesses.

A statement from the coroner and sheriff of Cochise County, Arizona Territory, had been signed by the fourteen citizens who had viewed the remains of Ringo's body. They indicated that it was propped up in a sitting position when it was discovered, "facing west, the head inclined to the right." The only wound in the body was a "part of the scalp gone including a small portion of the forehead and part of the hair." The coroner's inquest said that Ringo had died from a gunshot wound, but stated that the actual *cause* of death could not be determined. The newspaper later revealed that the hole was "large enough to admit two fingers about halfway between the right eye and ear, and a hole correspondingly large on top of his head, doubtless the outlet of the fatal bullet."

Ringo's feet had been wrapped in a torn undershirt, although he did not appear to have walked any distance in that manner. In his hand was a colt .45 SAA revolver. A new Winchester model 1876 .45-60 rifle was found leaning against the same tree that supported its former owner. Mysteriously, one of Ringo's two cartridge belts, the one containing the .45 cartridges for his pistol, was found belted on his body upside-down.

The July 18, 1882, issue of the *Tombstone Epitaph,* in reporting Ringo's death, said that "many people who are intimately acquainted with him in life have serious doubts that he took his own life, while an equally large number say that he frequently threatened to commit suicide." The paper, it said, leaned toward the second theory.

On that same day the *Pueblo Daily Chieftain* revealed that I had been in Leadville on July 18—the first report of my whereabouts since I had last been seen in Salida on July 7. I was virtually cleared of playing any part in Johnny Ringo's death. With the Arizona murder warrant still hanging over my head, the paper speculated, I would have been a fool to have left the safe haven of Colorado for Arizona Territory, for *any* reason.

But what do papers know, anyway?

Months later, after it was all finished and justice had been rendered, Wyatt would look at me with those steel-blue eyes of his, nod his head, and smile. "Thanks, Doc," he would say to me. "Thanks for everything."

And I would know exactly what he meant.

One Last Goodbye

A number of historians believe that Johnny Ringo took his own life. Others believe that I had something to do with his untimely demise. After all, my relationship with Mr. Ringo over the years had been somewhat *checkered,* to say the least.

People who say that Ringo committed suicide point to the fact that the Pueblo County court records show I was in Pueblo, Colorado, at the time of his death, citing the *writ of capias* that the judge had rendered following my failure to appear as scheduled, and later in the day appearing in person—*in propera persona,* as the court recorder had noted, or "in his own proper person." A strike for my having been in Pueblo around the time of Ringo's death in Arizona.

But in a court of law, *in propera persona* is not taken literally. It means that *someone* appeared before the court on my behalf, but not necessarily yours truly. On that particular day, of course, it was my attorney who had appeared on my behalf, despite the wording of the court record, which is merely a standard legal filler text. A strike *against* my having been in Pueblo around the time of Ringo's death in Arizona.

Add the fact that the entire Pueblo charge for "larceny" was nothing more than a trumped-up matter created by Bat Masterson and some other friends as a convenient means of preventing me from being forcibly extradited to Arizona, and you begin to get the feeling that I may indeed not have felt the necessity to appear in court in Pueblo on that or on *any* day. Even if the authorities were unaware of the false nature of the charges at the time.

Of course, when I failed to appear in court, my attorney stood in for me, and the case was continued, ultimately to a date following Ringo's death. That combined with the general knowledge that I was in Salida on July 7, as reported by the local paper, means I could quite easily have met with Wyatt Earp and the others just west of town. I believe, in fact, that a woman by the name of Josie Marcus Earp attested to that very fact. Josie, you see, was the woman for whom Wyatt had fallen so wildly in love just as his relationship with Mattie was falling so wildly apart, the woman who recounted Wyatt's days as a frontiersman after his death. She knew as much about our activities, at least from Wyatt's point of view, as anyone alive.

The next time anyone documented my whereabouts was on July 18 in Leadville, the very date to which my bogus Pueblo case had been continued. Ringo's death had been reported on July 13, you understand, according to the lone woman who had heard a single shot echo up from the canyon.

Naturally, Wyatt took credit for Ringo's death. Some people suggest that he did so because he was, indeed, the man's executioner. Others point to the possibility that Wyatt was merely protecting me from any additional trumped-up charges that might be leveled at me had I been credited with the shooting. After all, Wyatt Earp had a badge; I had a cough.

The truth of the matter is that it might have been both of us who finally exterminated the vermin known as John Ringo. It might have been one of us who goaded him into drawing, while the other pulled his pistol out, held it upright, pulled back the hammer until it locked into place, and—some six or seven paces from the man—pulled the trigger as the sound of the polished nickel hammer striking the brass casing holding the powder and ball exploded, sending the ball whizzing through the air, through his scalp, and out the back of his head as quickly as all of that.

At least that is much the way I recall it having happened.

So far as my participation with the Earp boys and the others in bringing those responsible for murder to justice, I tell you this: A vendetta is a wonderful thing. It purges the soul of the inequities so often discovered there. It cleanses the heart and, while doing so, scrubs the blood clean.

And so it did with me. While I rode, hard, all across the Southwest, sleeping under the stars, sometimes in rain and sometimes in the frigid night air, followed by twelve or fourteen hours beneath the broiling sun, my consumption worsened, as would be expected. But my conditions took a turn for the better. My outlook on life was no longer confined to the rhapsody of death beating on the drums. It had been expanded to include the symphony of cause: The Earps had been legally empowered with removing the vilest elements of society from the ranks of social humanity, and I had been empowered as their aide.

It was not so petty a squabble, as history would later record it, as the "Earp-Clanton Feud." It was not a feud by any means. At least it was not from the Earps' point of view. It was a simple understanding of justice, humanity, and the West. When the evil forces take control of one's daily life, that life cannot help but be diminished, impoverished, and eventually snuffed out prematurely—figuratively and literally. The western frontier had developed more rapidly than the very society empowered to embrace it. When that happens, injustice is sure to prevail. Righting that injustice is imperative for the survival of humanity. And that is exactly what the Earp party set about doing.

When we rode out of Tombstone that evening, we had made a pledge to one another. We pledged to fight for justice, no matter where, no matter how. When the laws of man fail to provide a platform, the laws of right prevail.

The laws of right were on our side. That is one of the reasons I felt so damned good about the entire affair. That is one of the reasons I believed my battle with my cursed disease was abating. That I was winning.

Oh, the coughing was still there, of course. But it nearly always abated with the administration of libidinous spirits. Whisky is a great emancipator.

And then something happened that changed all that. I was living in Leadville at the time. It had been a sleepy little mountain village until 1877, when the discovery of a rich outcropping of silver ore turned it into a boomtown. Overnight it exploded in size, population, and notoriety. I could not resist the call, let alone the temptation.

I was asleep around three in the morning when I heard a tremendous explosion that rocked my bed. By the time I got up and looked out the window, the Texas House—the classiest gambling hall in town—was engulfed in flames. I threw on my clothes, grabbed my hat, and raced downstairs and out into the street, where the firemen were already hard at work trying to remove people from the place, which was open twenty-four hours a day. I watched as a couple firemen who had collapsed from the smoke and heat had to be removed from the building, and the mayor or someone ran over to the hall to start the bell ringing for reinforcements.

Well, being right there already, I saw no value to gawking, so I grabbed a pail and joined in a brigade, which several others were beginning to form. After several hours of slinging water at the blaze, we finally managed to get the fire out, but the building was lost. Burned to cinders and smoldering rubble, both the structure and all of its furnishings. Nothing remained of value.

Remarkably, no one was killed, and we managed to prevent the fire from spreading to the neighboring buildings. Since it was nearly sunup by then, I decided to get some breakfast at a saloon just down the street. And something to wash it down with. And to lick my wounds. My lungs burned, my body ached. I coughed all throughout my meal. I went back to my room to try to get some rest, but instead I hacked away, bringing up a whole new array of colorful phlegm—gray, mostly, with streaks of yellow and green and blue. Blue, can you imagine? And red, of course. Lots and lots of deep brownish-colored red.

I apologize for being so graphic, for my intent is not to cause you disgust or vexation, I assure you. But I would hope to impress upon you that, from that moment on, I knew deep down inside that my disease was no longer in remission.

If, indeed, it ever *had* been.

As the days passed, I found myself losing weight. The clothes I had carried with me for most of my adult life hung on me like a damp bed sheet on a line, drying in the sun. The image in the mirror staring back at me mornings looked pale, gaunt, and tired.

And I was tired. If truth be known, I was tired of the disease, tired of the struggle, tired of not having enough money—for, you see, as the disease progressed, so too did my drinking, which gave me some modicum of respite. With my increased drinking came a decreased capacity to think. And with that came a losing streak at faro the likes of which substantially set me back financially.

I still practiced dentistry whenever I could find someone ignorant enough or simplistic enough to allow me into his mouth—mostly a spur-of-the-moment occasion when someone had lost a tooth in a brawl or dropped a filling while biting into an olive or the like. I had no dental practice, of course, no office, nothing of the sort, so I would do the extraction or whatever else was required of the occasion in my room above the saloon. How very convenient. I was never at a loss for anesthesia.

My weight continued to decline dramatically over the next several days; my physical condition was less than ideal. I made it a point to befriend a local chemist, Jay Miller, who worked at the apothecary at the corner of Sixth Street and Harrison. He was a good, gentle, and kindly soul, and when the whiskey no longer satisfied my needs as a painkiller, he would provide to me, free of charge, as much laudanum as I required.

Now, being a doctor, I knew the effects of opiates, and I knew that the prospects for recovery from extended reliance upon them were meager. I had seen laudanum used effectively as a pain reliever for years; but I had rarely seen it used by someone who recovered from his condition, stopped his reliance on the drug, and went on to become a fully functioning productive member of society. That's not how laudanum works.

A combination of opium and grain alcohol—the alcohol was added to the opium to make it somewhat more palatable and to increase the speed of the numbing effects of the drug—laudanum was just about the last resort for pain the medical professional possessed.

I was not pleased when I found myself drawn to it for relief, I promise you. Yet, despite what I knew of the drug and the people who took it, the outcome of their treatments, and the depth of the graves into which their tired and lifeless bodies were eventually settled, I could not resist. The pain of doing so, the physical pain, the burning and sharp stabbing pain to my lungs and my chest, the pain to my back and my head from coughing continually—deep and guttural and endless coughing—were all too much for a simple country boy from Georgia to bear.

And so, laudanum.

I was in a conundrum. I did not know which way to turn for help. I was beginning to feel that there was no way out. That one morning soon, I would awaken to my coughing, take my usual half bottle or so of whisky—or more likely a deep pull on the laudanum—and go back to sleep, this time forever.

It must have been how my mother had felt in her final hours. The coughing and hacking and wheezing had been enormous. Coming and going, I thought she was simply having a bad spell and that, as always, she would eventually supplant it with a healthy spell that, with Godspeed, would see her through her disease once and for all.

It never did.

So I waited and I hoped and I wondered, and the last thing in the world I looked forward to was a visit from two old acquaintances from Arizona Territory stopping by to see me.

Let me explain.

Back in Tombstone, at the shootout, there was a man by the name of William "Billy" Allen who was associated with Ike Clanton. Just prior to the fight, he and Reuben Coleman had walked down Allen Street through the O. K. Corral to the front of Camilius Fly's Gallery behind the boarding house. Once the lead started flying, I swear to God, I heard shots coming from the buildings lining the street. Shots that could only have been fired at Wyatt and me and the others by Allen.

Now, suddenly, Allen had come to Leadville, this time in the company of Johnny Tyler, still nursing the humiliation he had suffered in 1880 when Wyatt Earp had ejected him physically from Tombstone's Oriental Saloon as I looked on. I may have thrown a verbal taunt or two after him in the process. I can't recall.

Now they were both in Leadville. And they were both looking for a fight.

They got together several of their cronies to call upon me in Hyman's bar, where I frequently settled afternoons and evenings. After seeing me in my weakened condition, they began taunting me, finally advising me to pull my gun. I told them that I was not heeled, and it was true. Since coming to Leadville, I had been stopped and frisked on numerous occasions by the local police and made sure that, in order to avoid any more costly skirmishes with the law, I remained on the right side of the town's founding fathers.

The local paper heard of the incident, and after sending a reporter to interview me, wrote: "[The Tyler faction were] would-be bad men" and asserted that "this much to be said for Holliday—he has never since his arrival here made any 'bad breaks' or conducted himself in any other way than a quiet peaceable manner."

Nonetheless, I had at one point in a game of poker found myself with an exceptionally good hand and no funds with which to back it, so, borrowing $5 from Billy Allen, I promised to repay the debt within a week. Well, the hand turned out to be less good than I had originally thought, and when the week expired, so too did Allen's generosity toward me. He told me to pay the debt by the next day or be prepared for trouble.

When that Tuesday arrived with the money still absent, I asked a friend of mine to go down to the saloon and conceal my Colt .41

revolver at the end of the bar, near the cigar case, which he did. I entered the bar some while later, and when Billy Allen followed, I saw his hand in his pocket. Knowing that he was itching for a fight—and anxious to become the one and only man to shoot down Doc Holliday—I grabbed the pistol from behind the bar and fired. The shot struck the blackguard in the fleshy part of the upper arm, severing an artery. As he fell to the floor, I fired again, missing his head by mere inches. Before I could pull a third round, the bartender grabbed me, and a policeman who had been stationed outside burst in.

Of course, I was arrested, charged with attempted murder, and scheduled for trial.

Would this be it? I wondered. Would this, after all the trials I had endured, after all the charges, trumped up and otherwise—would this be the one to bring Doc Holliday to his heels?

When the preliminary hearing began and the prosecutor had presented his evidence, my attorney called upon me to testify. After explaining the part about the loan and the threat, I told the jury, "I saw Allen coming in with his hand in his pocket, and I thought my life was as good to me as his was to him; I fired the shot, and he fell on the floor, and [I] fired the second shot; I knew that I would be a child in his hands if he got hold of me; I weigh 122 pounds; I think Allen weighs 170; I have had the pneumonia three or four times; I don't think I was able to protect myself against him."

I thought it a most eloquent and fitting speech. The jury did not. They decided there was enough evidence to remand me to custody pending a trial for premeditated murder. Judge Rice increased my bail to $8,000 and ordered me imprisoned pending my raising of the additional $3,000 bail. I finally managed to do so on September 6. The trial date had been set for November.

As the Holliday family luck would have it, on March 28, 1885, following the trial of one Doctor John Henry Holliday, the jury, after a short deliberation, returned a verdict of not guilty. After seven months of waiting, I was finally a free man once more.

Free.

Except for the damage to my lungs that the cold, harsh conditions of both the jail and of the town of Leadville itself, in the rarified environment of the Rocky Mountains, had done to me.

I decided to escape the impending harsh winter of 1885–86 by traveling from Leadville to Denver, where I spent several months. I confess to frequenting both the Arcade and the Argyle saloons, as well as Patrick O'Connell's Missouri House on Blake Street.

That May I heard that the great Wyatt Earp had come to Denver, and I sent word that I wanted to meet with him at the Windsor Hotel. Wyatt arrived right on time, in the company of his new bride, Josephine (or "Sadie," as he had nicknamed her—his Tombstone infatuation). Josie later left her accounting of our meeting:

> There coming toward us was Doc Holliday, a thinner, more delicate-appearing Doc Holliday than I had seen in Tombstone. I have never seen a man exhibit more pleasure at meeting a mere friend than Doc did. "When I heard you were in Denver, Wyatt, I wanted to see you once more," he said, "for I can't last much longer. You can see that."
>
> They chatted for a few minutes, then he and Wyatt walked away, Doc on visibly unsteady legs. My husband was deeply affected by this parting from a man who, like an ailing child, had clung to him as though to derive strength from him. There were tears in Wyatt's eyes when at last they took leave of each other. Doc threw his arm across his shoulder.
>
> "Goodbye, old friend," he said. "It will be a long time before we meet again."
>
> He turned and walked away as fast as his feeble legs would permit.

After wintering in Denver I moved on to Silverton, where I had heard another strike had been made and yet more fortunes remained to be made. But neither rumor turned out to be true, and by summer late I had returned again to Denver, where I took up residence at the

Metropolitan Hotel on Sixteenth Street. The local constabulary was not happy to learn of my arrival. To them—and I cannot blame them one bit—I was trouble waiting to happen. They let it be known that my life would be easier and much more pleasant if I moved elsewhere.

So, I returned to Leadville, where I went into partnership with my old friend Mannie Hyman. But my health continued to worsen, and my spirits along with it, until the point came when I was so low I could not imagine what to do next.

I wrote to Kate at the hotel in Globe, telling her that I had decided to go on to Glenwood Springs to take of the curative sulfur springs there. And I asked her to join me. It was not an easy thing for me to do. Kate and I had not corresponded for months, and I was not even sure that she would reply to me, let alone entertain my notion. But I felt so alone, so depressed, so despondent and desperate. It is a bad thing to say, I know, and I beg your forgiveness. But to me at that unctuous point in my life, I had no alternative. Anything would have been better than what I had allowed myself. Even Kate, whose reaction to my failed health I could not possibly imagine, would have been better. Even that.

So, I arrived via stagecoach in Glenwood Springs in May 1887. I immediately attempted to set up a dental practice but failed. My cough was by then far too violent and unrestrained to allow me to work. I did apply for and receive employment from Judd Riley to help guard a coal claim at a nearby mine, which paid $10 a day. By the time that work had ended, Kate had arrived.

I did not know how I would react to seeing her again.

Or how she would to me.

But I soon enough found out.

She hugged me, kissed me on the cheek, stepped back and looked at me closely, something I had hoped she would not do, and shrank at the sight. "What have you done to yourself, Doc?" she demanded.

"Why, darling," I told her. "I have often assented that, without you in my life, I would shrivel away to nothing."

The words were glib. Her reaction was anything but. She immediately set upon contacting her brother, Alexander, to use his cabin in nearby Penny Hot Springs in Crystal Valley, where he, his wife Eva, and Kate could best care for me. But their attempts failed to turn the stars in the sky, and we soon decided to return to Glenwood Springs and its mineral baths. It was my only hope.

So once again in Springs, Kate and I took a room at the Hotel Glenwood, just half a block from the mineral waters, on the corner of Grand Avenue and Eighth Street. The hotel was the finest in the entire Rocky Mountains, boasting both electrical lighting and hot and cold running water in every room.

I took to playing faro in several of the gambling houses in town, although the sulfur vapors generated by the hot springs had a decidedly debilitating effect on my consumptive lungs. The town itself was lovely; the residents, quite accommodating. They all knew who I was, and they all bent over backwards to make Kate and me feel at home.

But in the end, it wasn't enough.

On Wednesday, October 5, 1887, the first Denver and Rio Grande Railroad spur opened in Glenwood, with all the expectant hoopla and celebration. I, alas, was not healthy enough to attend. In fact, I had become bedridden several weeks prior.

Kate, God bless her wayward soul, stayed with me round-the-clock. She gave me my laudanum, tried to comfort my melancholia, and in all respects played the role of perfect salvaging angel to my Satan.

I, on the other hand, continued to weaken until the point that I could no longer work, no longer eat, no longer drink. The many years of late hours, rough liquor, thin air, pneumonia, and tuberculosis had finally caught up with me. The last fifty-seven days of my life were spent confined to bed, during which period I rose only twice. The bellhop served us our meals so that Kate would not need to leave my side.

My funds were exhausted, and Kate in her magnitude dipped into her own savings to see us through.

Finally, I had become delirious. On Monday, November 7, I found myself unable to speak. I would look up at Kate, at her angelic features and smooth clear skin, recall what my own pasty white emaciated face had looked like for the past thirty-five years of my life, and marvel at her beauty, inside and out. I would think to myself how lucky I was. To have had her. By my side. When she could have and, by all logical conveyances of humankind, *should* have left me cold. And then, at ten o'clock on the morning of November 8, 1887, I died in our room at the Hotel Glenwood of miliary tuberculosis.

For Doctor John Henry Holliday, dentist extraordinaire, the fight was finally over.

EPILOGUE

The story of Doc Holliday is a complicated one in many ways. How do you tell the tale of a man who has suffered pain along every step of life's walk, from his birth as a malformed young child to his death as an alcoholic disease-riddled thirty-six-year-old man, without having it sound maudlin?

Yet, in many ways, my life was richer and fuller than the lives of people three times my age. But for my own spirit of adventure, brought about by the necessity of my having to leave my beloved home in Georgia for my own health, I might never have known the beauty and love to which I was ultimately exposed. Certainly I never would have known Kate. Nor would my path have crossed that of Wyatt, Morgan, and the other Earp boys and their families.

Kate and I, of course, had enjoyed a tumultuous relationship. Not the most physically attractive woman in the world, she nonetheless possessed a set of full features that satisfied me carnally on numerous occasions, particularly when we were young. Just watching her undress almost always caught my attention.

But our physical relationship soon began to pall as I succumbed to the dulling effects of alcohol and, later, laudanum. Still, my love for her was true and unwavering, as I realize hers was for me, in her own way.

In one manner of speaking, we were both of us soiled doves. She, by the very nature of her profession, which had been literally forced upon her from a young age; and me, by the very nature of the beast that ate away at me from the inside out. What better combination of persons to find and to cling to one another through each other's most trying times?

In the Earp brothers I found a camaraderie and a love I had known for no one since those days of innocent pleasures enjoyed by my cousin Robert and me. I found in the Earps the family I'd once had and lost. In Virg, a replacement for the father who had abandoned me to the forces of lust and ambition simply because it became expedient to do so. In Morg, the good friend I had once known and lost to the ravages of time and distance. In Wyatt, the morality and the scruples I have always admired and feared I would never possess.

In my cousin Mattie, for whom I had once bequeathed my undying love, I found the admiration of a lifetime. She went on to join the Catholic Church and eventually entered the Order of the Sisters of Mercy. She died of natural causes, Sister Mary Melanie, a devoted teacher and tender caregiver. And I shall always be indebted to her moral support and the sustenance she showed her wayward cousin throughout his most trying years.

To my other relatives, my uncles and aunts and cousins—well, I only hope they understood that, because my illness and my pride prevented me from staying close by them, they were never far from me in my heart. I wish now that things had worked out differently for me and that I had managed to retain the strong bonds formed with them, particularly with the McKey side of the family. But we do not always get to see things through the way we might desire.

To my mother—well, what can I say? She was always there for me when I needed her, never far from my side. I tried as best I could to return the compliment as she grew weaker and less able to perform the familial duties to which she longed so desperately to return.

To my own disease, as strange as it may sound, I realize at last I owe a debt of gratitude perhaps larger than any other. It made me recognize just how gallantly my mother had fought in those failing years of life, just how painfully she had struggled. She was the love that formed our family, created it, and bound it together for as long as she was physically able. But for my own contraction, I might never have realized how much she loved us, and me.

And so it is that, with the passage of this story of the true life and times of one Doctor John H. Holliday to whoever might find it to be of some fleeting interest, I would hope to return to the side of those dear ones whom I valued most in life. It has been a long journey.

But the telling of the truth shall set you free. And I am forever hopeful that, with the unleashing of this tale, I will at last enjoy the freedom so long denied me.

And that the bonds that held me captive will be broken at last forever.

Verbum Sapienti.

INDEX

A

Adams, Andy, 98–99
alcohol, 74, 87, 99, 112, 169
Allen, William "Billy," 170–72
Arizona Mail and Stage
    Company (Kinnear) holdup,
    58, 118–21, 122
arrests and indictments
    attempted murder, 64,
        75–76, 172
    avoiding extradition to
        Tombstone, 159, 166
    disorderly conduct, 82, 115–16
    gambling, 71, 76–77, 78, 83,
        102, 106, 110
    larceny, 160–61
    murder, 90–91, 140, 151–52,
        156–59
    purpose of, 110
    stage robbery attempt and
        murder, 122, 123
    threats against lives, 121–22
    weapons possession, 110, 142
Atlantic & Gulf Railroad, 42
Austin, Charles W., 64, 75–76

B

Bailey, Ed, 80, 89–91
Barnes, Johnny, 152
Bassett, Charlie, 97, 98, 99
Beehive, 77–78, 87
Beeson, Chalk, 97

Behan, John H. "Johnnie"
    arrest warrants, 151–52, 153,
        154, 156–60
    description, 57–58
    Elder affidavit and, 122
    newspaper letter on, 158
    O.K. Corral gunfight, xiii–xiv,
        55–56, 133–36, 139, 140
    stage holdup and, 119,
        120–21, 123
Bella Union Saloon, 68, 71
Belle (whore), 49
Berry, George A. B., 144, 146
blacks, 17, 30, 37, 44
Boot Hill, 96
Boyle, Ned, 130
Breackenridge, William, 119
Breckenridge, Texas, 81–82
Bridges, Jack, 99
Brocius, Curly Bill, 57, 58, 120,
    142, 152, 161
buffalo, 95, 96
Byers, Billy, 125

C

*California: For Health, Pleasure
    and Residence* (Nordholl), 62
Campbell & Hatch's, 146
Carroll, Patrick, 78
Cattle Exchange Saloon, 84
cattle industry, 94, 96–97

cattle rustlers, 57–58, 83. *See also* Cowboys
Cherokee War, 10–11
Civil War
  black enlistees, 31
  defeat of South, 31–32, 33–34, 36
  effects and aftermath, 30–31, 46
  Holliday family and, 19–22, 29, 32–33
  issues of, 16–18
  Southern attitude toward, 18–19
Claiborne, William "Billy," 131–32, 136–39
Clanton, Billy, xiii–xiv, 56, 57, 133, 134–39, 140
Clanton, Ike
  as Behan posse member, 152
  O.K. Corral gunfight, xii–xiv, 56, 57, 58, 130–32, 136–39
  reward plot, 124, 128–30
  stage holdup suspect, 120
  in Tucson, 151
  vendettas, 142, 145
Clanton, Old Man, 57, 125
Clanton, Phin, 57
Coleman, Reuben, xiii–xiv, 133, 171
Collins, "Shotgun," 99
Comstock, Sylvester, 139
consumption (pulmonary tuberculosis)
  associates with, 59

dentistry profession affected by, 68, 72–73
diagnosis, 60–62
family history of, 26–27
gratitude toward, 178
health condition, 99, 100–101, 118, 167–70, 173, 174–75
self-medication, 74, 99, 112, 169
treatments, 62, 100, 101, 112, 169–70, 175
courthouse bombing plans, 46–47
Cowboy Band, 97
Cowboys
  arrests, 126
  assassinations, 143–49
  background and members, 57
  bounties and rewards on, 124
  hideouts, 123
  O.K. Corral gunfight, xii–xv, 56, 57, 128–39
  shootouts with posses, 125
  stagecoach robberies, 58, 118–21, 122
  trial outcome and death threats, 141–42
  vendettas and shootings, 124
Crane, Jim, 119, 121, 123, 124, 125
Cruz, Indian Charlie Florentino, 145, 149, 152

D

Dallas, Texas, 62–65, 67, 68, 71
Dallas County Fair exhibition awards, 66–67

Davis, Jefferson, 31
death rumors, 82
death threats, 141–42
Denison, Texas, 72
Deno, Lottie, 87–88
dentistry
    Dallas practice, 51, 53, 62,
        65–66, 70–71, 72–73
    dental assistant positions, 50
    Dodge City practice, 98, 99
    education, 45–48, 49–50
    Glenwood Springs
        practice, 174
    Leadville practice, 169
Denver, Colorado, 76, 77, 173
Denver Republic, interviews
    with, 158
"Diseases of the Teeth"
    (thesis), 50
disorderly conduct arrests, 82,
    115–16
Dodge City, Kansas, 94–96,
    98–99
Dodge House, 94, 98
Donnelly, Owen, 77–78
drinking, 74, 87, 99, 112, 169
duels, 42
dying with boots on, 5

E
Earp, Allie, 107, 149
Earp, Bessie, 52–53, 84, 85, 150
Earp, James, 57, 85, 107, 109,
    113, 144, 150
Earp, Josephine Marcus "Josie,"
    4, 121, 166, 173

Earp, Lou, 113, 150
Earp, Mattie, 4, 89, 98, 107, 147,
    148, 150, 166
Earp, Morgan
    assassination of, 143–49
    Crane posse, 125
    friendship with, 178
    Kinnear stage holdup
        posse, 119
    O.K. Corral gunfight, xii–xv,
        126–27, 134, 135, 136–39
    in Tombstone, 57, 109, 113
Earp, Sallie, 84
Earp, Virgil
    assassination attempts, 141–42
    brother's assassination, 144
    Cowboy arrests, 126
    friendship with, 178
    as law officer, xi, 113, 129
    O.K. Corral gunfight, xii–xv,
        57, 130–39
    in Tombstone, 107, 129
    vendetta target, 149
Earp, Warren, 125, 144, 147, 148
Earp, Wyatt
    Arizona strike, 106–7
    arrest warrants for, 151–52
    assassination attempts, 144
    Bailey killing, 80, 90, 92
    Behan and, 121
    Behan's attempted arrest of,
        151–52
    brother's assassination, 144,
        146–49
    Clanton arrest and threat,
        130–31

Cowboy reward plot, 124–25,
128–29
description, 100
on Doc's weaponry skills, 74
friendship with, 4–5, 75, 89,
100, 111, 129–30, 178
last visit with, 173
as law officer, 97, 98, 99,
113, 124
on Leonard, 117–18
life-saving incidents, 100
O.K. Corral gunfight, xii–xv,
55–57, 128–29, 132–40
saloon investment, 114
sheriff election, 57–58, 121
shootist skills of, 112
as shotgun messenger, 113
vendettas for brother's
assassination, 148, 149,
150–54, 161, 162–66
Elder, "Big Nose" Kate (Mary
Katherine Harony; Kate
Fisher)
affidavits implicating Doc,
122, 123
aliases, 51, 84
autobiographical fantasies, 52
background, 51, 84
career, 84–85
as caretaker during last days,
174–76
description, 85
in Dodge City, 94
in Globe, 113, 123, 141, 150
jail escapes, 91–92
in Las Vegas, 100–102, 106

relationship with, 85–87, 177
rivals, 87–89
shootist reputation promoted
by, 111–12
in Tombstone, 107, 122,
125–26, 127
Ernshaw, Harry, 125

F
faro, 60, 68–69, 73, 84, 88, 114
fights, 114, 122
fires, 67, 71, 91, 168
Fisher, Kate (actress), 51
Fisher, Kate (prostitute). *See*
Elder, "Big Nose" Kate
Flynn, James, 142
Fogarty, Mike, 87, 88
Ford, Arthur C., 53, 59, 62
Fort Dodge, Kansas, 95
Fort Griffin, Texas, 77–78, 83–84
Foy, Eddie, 103
Freedmen's Bureau, 37, 46
Freis, John Doe, 149
Frink, Lucian Frederick, 50
Fuches, A. Jameson, Jr., 51
Fuller, Wes, 137

G
gambling
and altercations, 114
arrests for, 71, 76–77, 78, 83,
102, 106
assessment ordinances, 110
in Dodge City, 97, 98
drinking affecting, 169
in Fort Griffin, 84, 88

fraud (cheating), 69, 74, 82,
  90, 114
games of choice, 73
lawmen participation, 98
legislation prohibiting, 102
as profession, 68–70
and self-defense, 74, 82,
  89–91, 111
in Tombstone, 114
training, 60
Georgia, State of, 16
Glenwood Springs, Arizona,
  174–75
Golden, Johnny, 87
Goodrich, Briggs, 145
Gordon, Mike, 93, 104–5
Grant, Ulysses S., 32
Gray, Dick "Dixie," 123, 125
Gray, Mike, 123
guns, 54, 74, 75, 97, 110, 111–12
Gus (saloon), 87

H

habeas corpus writs, 156–57,
  159–60
Hape, Samuel, 62
Harony, Mary Katherine. *See*
  Elder, "Big Nose" Kate
Haslett, Bill and Ike, 123, 124
Head, Harry the Kid, 119, 121,
  123, 124
Hidalgo, Francisco, 11, 20, 60
Hill, Joe, 124
Holliday, Alice Jane (McKey)
  (mother), 11, 14, 26–27, 29,
  35, 38–40, 178–79

Holliday, George Henry, 20, 69,
  82–83
Holliday, Henry Burroughs
  (father)
early years, 10–11
marriage and family life, 11–
  12, 14–15
military service, 21, 24, 29–30
political career, 81
property lawsuit, 41
property sales and purchases,
  19, 32–33, 36
during Reconstruction, 37, 46
second marriage, 40–41
Holliday, John Henry "Doc"
birth, 12
character, 1–3, 36, 85, 158
childhood, 13–15, 19, 22–28,
  40–42
death, 5–7, 176
description, 1, 13–14, 65–66,
  81, 157, 161
early employment, 42, 50
education, 36, 45–48, 49–50
employment, 102–4, 174 (*see
  also* dentistry)
family background, 10–12
health, 12–13 (*see also*
  consumption)
as lawman, 99
love interests, 34–35, 178 (*see
  also* Elder, "Big Nose" Kate)
religion, 67
as saloon owner, 105–6
shootist skills and reputation,
  74, 75, 111–12

Holliday, John Stiles, 12, 20, 23, 45, 50, 60–61, 62
Holliday, Martha Eleanora, 11–12
Holliday, Mary Elizabeth (Wright), 82
Holliday, Mattie, 34–35, 60, 81, 178
Holliday, Mollie, 34
Holliday, Permelia, 12, 15, 45, 50, 62
Holliday, Rebecca (Burroughs), 10
Holliday, Robert Alexander, 10, 31
Holliday, Robert "Hub," 15, 23–24, 45, 62, 81
Holliday, Robert Kennedy, 20, 34, 36, 44, 45, 59–60
Holliday Saloon, 105–6, 107
Hooker, Henry C., 153
Hyman, Mannie, 174

I
Iron Front Building, 41, 53, 60

J
Jacobs, Henry, 78, 83
Jacobs, John, 88
jail escapes, 91–92
Jesus Christ, 2
Johnson, Turkey Creek Jack, 150, 151, 152, 155
Josie (prostitute), 49
Joyce, Milton E., 56, 57, 108–9, 115, 117, 121, 122, 156

K
Kahn, Henry, 82
King, Luther, 119, 120, 121
Kinnear (Benson) stage holdups, 58, 118–21, 122

L
Lang, William, 125
larceny arrests, 160–61
Larn, John M., 83
Las Vegas, New Mexico Territory, 100, 101–2, 104
laudanum, 112, 169–70
Leonard, William, 58, 117–18, 119, 120, 121, 123, 124
Leslie, Frank, 119
Lincoln, Abraham, 18, 30
Linton, Charles T., 159
Long, Crawford, 13
Lucas, J. H., 140
Lungers' Club, 101
Lynch, Mike, 78

M
MacVeigh, Isaac W., 124
Mallen, Perry M., 155–56, 157–58, 159, 160
Martin, Rachel, 40
Masterson, Bat
   description, 100
   Doc's arrest and defense, 156, 158, 159
   on Doc's reputation, 75
   El Moro visit with, 155
   on Gordon killing, 105

Kinnear holdup posse
  member, 119
  as law officer, 97, 98, 99, 102–3
  race attendance with, 156
Masterson, Ed, 98, 99
Masterson, Jim, 98, 99
Mather, "Mysterious" Dave,
  99, 104
McCarty, Thomas, 97–98
McCoin, Rebecca Annaleezie
  (Holliday), 81
McKey, James Taylor, 20
McKey, Thomas Sylvester, 20, 41,
  42–43, 44, 50–51
McLaury, Frank, xii–xiv, 57, 124,
  133–39, 140
McLaury, Tom, xii–xiv, 57, 130,
  131, 132, 134–39, 140
McLaury, Will, 140, 142
McMasters, Sherman, 150, 151,
  152, 155
Melvin, Silas, 52
Miller, Jay, 169
murders
  accusations of, 157
  attempted, 64, 75–76, 172
  excusable homicides, 80, 89–
    91, 93, 104–5
  stage holdups and accusations
    of, 120–21
  vendettas for Morgan Earp
    assassination, 150–54,
    162–67
Murray, William B., 133–34

N
Nordholl, Charles, 62

O
O.K. Corral gunfight
  aftermath, 141–49
  arrests and trial, 140–41
  description, 136–39
  Earp, Wyatt, deposition, 55–57
  events leading to, 128–36
  injuries and death toll, 139–40
  newspaper accounts of, xi–xv
Oriental Saloon (Dallas), 75
Oriental Saloon (Tombstone), 57,
  108–9, 114–15, 146, 171
Osgood, Sam, 156

P
Parker, William C., 115
Parsons, George, 121, 142
Paul, Bob, 118, 119, 159, 160
Pennsylvania College of Dental
  Surgery, 47–48
Penny Hot Springs, 175
Philpott, Eli Bud, xii, 119
Pitkin, Frederick W., 158
Planters Hotel, 84
poker, 70, 73, 80
Prescott, Arizona, 107, 109–10

R
Reconstruction, 46, 50
red-light district (term), 95
Riley, Judd, 174
Ringo, Johnny, 57, 142, 145, 152,
  162–67

Royal Gorge War, 103–4

S

Santa Fe Railroad, 95, 102–3, 104

Santa Fe Trail, 94–95

Schwartz, Jack, 84

secession, 16–18

Seegar, John A., 62, 65–67, 70, 71–72

Selman, John Henry, 83

Shannsey, John, 84, 89

Sherman, William Tecumseh, 32, 33–34

Shibell, Charles, 133

shooting injuries, xiii, xiv, 82–83, 125

shootings. *See also* O.K. Corral gunfight

in Breckenridge, 82–83

at Devil's Kitchen, 125

in Las Vegas, 93, 104–5, 111

at Oriental Saloon (Tombstone), 108–9, 115, 117

shootist skills and reputation, 74, 75, 111–12

Silver City, New Mexico Territory, 154–55

Sitler, Henry L., 95

slavery, 17, 30

Smith, Lee, 158

Snow, Charles Bud, 125

Spanish monte, 73

Spencer, Marietta, 149

Spencer, Pete, xi–xii, 58, 120, 126, 149, 152

Spicer, Wells, 123, 140–41

springs, hot, 101, 174, 175

St. Charles saloon, 68

stagecoach robberies, xi, 58, 118–21, 122

stickpins, diamond, 62–63, 94

Stilwell, Frank, xi–xii, 58, 120, 126, 142, 145, 149, 150–51, 161

stinker (term), 95

Swilling, Hank, 142

T

Taylor, Zachary, 11

Thomas, George, 31

Thompson, Ben, 103

Thurmond, Frank (*aka* Mike Fogarty), 87, 88

Tilghman, Bill, 97, 99

Tin Hat Brigade, 83

Tipton, Dan, 145, 146, 153, 154

Tombstone. *See also* O.K. Corral gunfight

assassinations, 143–44

move to, 107, 113

post-gunfight climate, 141–42

saloon shootings, 57, 108–9, 114–15

sheriff election, 56–57, 121

stagecoach holdups and accusations, 118–21

Tombstone Epitaph, letters to, 153–54

Tompkins, Carlotte, 87–88

Tritle, Frederick A., 159, 160

tuberculosis, pulmonary. *See*
    consumption
Tyler, John, 108, 114, 171

V
Valdosta, Georgia, 32–33
Varnedoe, Samuel McWhir, 36
Venable, James M., 13
vendettas, 148, 149, 150–54,
    162–67
Vermilion, Texas Jack, 152, 155
vigilantes, 83–84

W
Wagner, Jack, 98
Walker, Alf, 98
Wallace, Albert, 131, 142
Wallace, Elbert O., 121
Webb, Jordan J., 105
Webster, A. B., 99
White, Charlie, 111, 161
whores and whorehouses, 48–49,
    51–53, 87. *See also* Elder,
    "Big Nose" Kate
Williams, Marshall, 119
Woods, Harry, 120–21

ABOUT THE AUTHOR

D. J. Herda is an award-winning author, photojournalist, editor, videographer, and artist with more than eighty books and several hundred thousand short stories, articles, columns, and scripts to his credit. His photography and art are included in private collections around the world. He presently lives and works out of his home in the southwestern United States.